AN OUTLINE HIS
EUROPEAN I

An outline history of European Music

MICHAEL HURD

With illustrations by John Miller

NOVELLO
London and Sevenoaks
Cat. No. 11 0139
ISBN 0 85360 076 7

PRINTED IN GREAT BRITAIN BY
HALSTAN & CO. LTD.,
AMERSHAM, BUCKS., ENGLAND

PREFACE

IN writing this book I have tried to take a panoramic view of musical history, such as may provide the serious student and music-lover with a sound framework upon which to base further, more detailed researches. It is not, and was never intended to be, an all-embracing account that will answer every question. Indeed, I very much doubt if any single volume by any one man should ever aspire to that end.

I have not, for example, included biographical sketches of important composers, nor indulged in analytical accounts of their music. There is literature enough, and to spare, to deal with such matters—as I have indicated in the bibliographical appendix. Instead, I have tried to answer the following questions:

> What was society like in each period, and what did it expect of its musicians?
> What were the main ingredients of music in each period, and what forms did that music take?
> Which were the most influential countries, and who were the most important composers?

If answers to these questions have been provided, and set down in a readable fashion, then I shall consider my purpose to have been fulfilled.

It follows, however, that the examination student, and the curious music-lover, will need to know more than this book sets out to provide. And to this end I have included suggestions for further reading, a possible course of listening, and a series of 'projects' designed to prompt more detailed lines of investigation. These are placed at the end of the book, so as not to break the flow of the narrative.

MICHAEL HURD

West Liss
Hampshire
July 1968

PREFACE TO THE SECOND EDITION

Any textbook which contrives to remain useful to students in schools, colleges, and universities for twenty years sooner or later requires revision, if only to catch up on recent developments. That revision, long overdue, has now been carried out.

Several innovations have been made. Chief among them is the provision of blank pages at the end of each historical section, so that additional personal notes may be added by the student. To the same end, space has been left after the birth date of each living composer, so that a final date may be added if and when the occasion arises.

The chapter 'Recent Experiments' has been completely rewritten, and the Appendices have been revised in such a way as to avoid the annoyance of being recommended books and records that are no longer readily available.

MICHAEL HURD

West Liss
Hampshire
January 1988

CONTENTS

INTRODUCTION

PART ONE: The Middle Ages. 1000-1400.

PART TWO: The Renaissance. 1400-1600.

CONTENTS

APPENDICES

MUSICAL EXAMPLES

INTRODUCTION

ALMOST everything we hear today as part of our regular musical diet was written after the year 1600. But this, of course, is not where European music began. To find any sort of beginning we must go back at least a thousand years. And even then we shall only be joining a story that has already begun. A complete history of music, if such were possible, would take us back, far beyond the oldest civilisation, to the earliest days of primitive man.

To go back a thousand years, however, is reasonable. For it was then that the basic pattern of modern Europe began to emerge from the chaos that followed the collapse of the Roman Empire. The Christian Church, the guiding light of the new civilisation, blossomed into something more than limited, local power. The intellectual life of Europe awoke, and architecture, art, literature, music, and philosophy all began to assert themselves as expressions of that new phenomenon: Western Man.

We shall go back, then, just over a thousand years: to AD 800, the year in which Charlemagne received the imperial crown of the Holy Roman Empire from the hands of Pope Leo III, and in so doing gave a sense of unity and direction to that vast tract of Europe which we now call France, Germany, and Italy. Although there were to be many changes in the years that followed, and many violent differences of opinion, the force of this symbolic act remained. Europe from that moment was able to build herself up as a Christian civilisation.

To have been a musician a thousand years ago would have meant one of two things. Either you would have been a minstrel, wandering from place to place, entertaining people with songs and dances, stories and tricks—turning your hand, in fact, to anything that might earn you a meal and a night's lodging. Or you would have been a monk, working in the peace and security of some great church or monastery, with music as part of the daily ritual of worship.

Of the two, only the monastic musician had the means and the encouragement to develop music as an art. The church must at this time be thought of as the sole guardian of learning and education, and thus the only haven in which artistic and intellectual pursuits might prosper. Inevitably, a history of music must concentrate its first attentions on the music of the church.

PART ONE

The Middle Ages

1000-1400

CHAPTER I

THE BEGINNINGS OF POLYPHONY

CHURCH music sprang from that collection of simple tunes which the early Christians used for chanting the various parts of their liturgy, and which we call PLAINSONG.

Although these tunes had been gathered from many different sources (some of them pagan) it was felt, as time went on, that they had a special religious significance. This feeling became even stronger when, at the end of the sixth century, Pope Gregory the Great completely overhauled the collection and laid down rules for singing it. From then on, plainsong (GREGORIAN CHANT) was regarded as being almost as holy as the words of the Bible itself.

Plainsong is pure melody. It needs no supporting harmony; and, unlike the music we are most accustomed to, it has no beat—no regular rhythm you can tap out with your foot. Instead, it seems to float: on and on in great arches of sound, endlessly.

It is precisely this floating, unworldly quality that makes it the perfect medium for religious words. And though solemn and restrained, and therefore in direct contrast with the wilder music of popular entertainment, it can still be enormously attractive to the listener. Indeed, its success was such that the early Church was accused of charming the people with magic chants.

Like all music up to about the year 1600, plainsong is written in one or other of the eight recognised CHURCH MODES.

A mode is simply a scale of consecutive notes. Our major and minor scales are both modes. But whereas every major scale keeps to a rigid pattern of distances between its notes (two large, one small; one large; two large, one small), the pattern changes for each church mode. The steps in one mode may appear as: one large, one small, three large, one small, one large; while in another mode they may be: one small, three large, one small, two large—and so on, through eight permutations.

The church modes were given Greek names and divided into pairs—the main (*authentic*) modes: Dorian, Phrygian, Lydian, and Mixolydian; and their dependent (*plagal*) modes: Hypodorian, Hypophrygian, Hypolydian, and Hypomixolydian. By the end of the sixteenth century four extra modes had been brought into practical use, and two more theorized about. But at the same time, however, the modal system also began to transform itself, as we shall see, into the major and minor scales that we use today.

There are three main types of plainsong melody. They can be recognised by the way in which the words are fitted to the notes. The simplest style we call SYLLABIC: one note is given to each syllable in the word. Next comes the NEUMATIC style: with a few notes to each syllable. And finally, the MELISMATIC: in which certain syllables are given a whole series of notes.

In very broad terms: the simplest of the three styles was used when the meaning of the words was all-important, while the fanciful, melismatic style was reserved for moments when emotions might legitimately spill out in terms of pure music (a word like 'Alleluia', for example, would attract this kind of treatment).

It is also true that the more complex styles represent a development and general flourishing in the art. The earlier and more persecuted the Christians, the simpler their style of chanting —for obvious reasons!

Catholic liturgy makes use of plainsong in the celebration of the MASS, and in the many smaller services known as CANONICAL HOURS—those moments of the day and night when the members of a monastic order assemble for prayers: Matins (midnight), Lauds (daybreak), Prime (6 am), Terce (9 am), Sext (midday), None (between 2 and 3 pm), Vespers (6 pm), and Compline (7 pm).

The final shape of the Mass was established by about the year 1000, and it provides for two kinds of liturgy. First there is the ORDINARY OF THE MASS, which includes the five parts that never change and which form the solid structure of the liturgy on every occasion. They are:

1. Kyrie (Lord, have mercy)
2. Gloria (Glory to God in the highest)
3. Credo (I believe in God)
4. Sanctus (Holy, holy, holy)
5. Agnus Dei (O Lamb of God)

Then there is the PROPER OF THE MASS, which adds those parts of the liturgy that change from day to day, according to the season or the saint. These include:

1.	Introit	The introduction to the service, sung as the priest enters.
2.	Gradual	The introduction preparatory to a reading from sacred texts.
3.	Alleluia	Brief interjections of praise, sung between the readings.
4.	Offertory	A processional chant sung while the people come to the altar to make their offerings.
5.	Communion	A processional chant sung as people come to take Holy Communion.

There are also two LESSONS proper to each Mass, and a variety of ACCLAMATIONS (Deo Gratias, Amen, etc), and, in penitential seasons, when the Alleluia is not sung, the TRACT. All of which go to make a complex and richly varied ritual, calling for a wide range of musical expression.

From the point of view of artistic development, the Church's desire to keep its collection of chants and sacred texts absolutely intact posed considerable problems. Fortunately, most composer-monks turned a blind eye to the Church's wishes. They were human, and their faith filled them with creative energy. In the end they simply could not help adding to the great treasury they had inherited.

This creative impulse led to the idea of TROPING—that is: the interpolation of new words and melodic phrases in the middle of old chants. Thus, a phrase such as 'Kyrie eleison' (Lord, have mercy) might be expanded into 'Kyrie Deus sempiterne eleison' (Lord, everlasting God, have mercy). These additions are known as TROPES.

The most important kind of trope is the SEQUENCE, the earliest examples of which date from the end of the ninth century. At first the sequence was not a musical invention at all, but merely an addition of words underneath certain of the more florid passages in the chants. For example: the last syllable in the word 'Gloria' might, in the original chant, be drawn out over a dozen or more notes. It seems to have been decided that phrases of this kind would be easier to remember if words were added beneath them. The new words, in turn, prompted the creation of whole poems, and these were eventually supplied with new music in their own right. In this way the sequence became a real trope—new words *and* new music growing out of the original chant.

The great centres of this art were the monasteries of St Gall (Switzerland) and St Marital (Limoges). And in later years the practice became so popular and exaggerated that the Vatican was forced to ban all but four of the most venerated sequences. Some idea of the heights this art could reach can be gained by a study of such long and beautiful poems as the *Dies Irae* by Thomas of Celano, and the *Stabat Mater* by Jacopone da Todi.

As part of the same stirring of creative activity we must add the first steps taken towards singing more than one melody at a time—the invention, that is, of POLYPHONY.

The first examples we have of this come from an anonymous treatise called *Musica Enchiriadis*, which dates from about the year 850. This shows how a chant (the VOX PRINCIPALIS could be sung at the same time as a new melody (the VOX ORGANALIS). In practice the 'new' tune mostly doubled the original chant at the interval of the fourth, or fifth, or octave, above or below—remaining in parallel with it all the time. This kind of polyphony is known as ORGANUM.

The fact that we first hear it mentioned in a text-book suggests that organum was already widely known. And it may well be that the Church was simply borrowing a style of singing that was in common use among ordinary people.

The idea of organum probably arose quite naturally out of several people with different ranges of voice all trying to sing the same tune. Soprano, alto, tenor, and bass voices lie roughly a fifth apart, so the kind of doubling we get in organum could occur spontaneously.

Nowadays, doubling a tune in parallel fourths, fifths, or octaves sounds a little bare and unsatisfactory. But we must remember that these intervals were the only ones that medieval ears could accept. By comparison, the thirds and sixths that later music enjoyed seemed impure and far too rich.

There are two kinds of organum: PARALLEL ORGANUM, in which the lines remain at a set distance from each other; and FREE ORGANUM, in which some variety of movement is introduced.

A further step was taken in the twelfth century. This involved the various parts moving not only in different directions from time to time, but also in different rhythms. Usually it meant that the chant was sung (or played) in long notes, while the added parts wove decorative melodies around it.

This advance, however, belongs properly to the next chapter. Before music could develop consistently it was necessary for someone to invent some method of writing it down. It may be perfectly easy for singers to remember their notes if they are all singing the same tune, but it is another matter when they all have different parts to sing.

The first attempts at writing music down were made about the year 600. This involved a number of signs called NEUMES, which were written above the words of the chant and served simply as reminders for singers who had already learned the music by heart. They showed, very roughly, whether the tune rose, or fell, or kept to the same note.

Some four hundred years later somebody decided to draw a single red line above the words of the chant. This line was to stand for the note F. Neumes that represented F itself could be placed on the line, while neumes for higher notes went above it, and neumes for lower notes went underneath.

From this it was but a short step to adding another line (a yellow one, for the note C), and then a third and a fourth. In this way a ladder, or STAVE, was created, with a step for each note of the scale. Once the performer had learned how to interpret the signs he could sing a new piece of music at sight.

The credit for perfecting this early form of notation is usually given to the monk Guido of Arezzo (c 995-1050).

The whole feeling of religious music up to about the year 1100 is one of dignity and uncomplicated strength. In this it is remarkably like the great cathedral architecture of the time. The Romanesque (Norman) style of building is more impressive in its structural grandeur than its decorative detail. And so it is with Gregorian Chant. Its composers were not much concerned to be original. They preferred to make inspired use of materials that had been handed down to them. It was not until the next century that the quest for originality began to make itself felt.

Although it does not affect the general style of the music, it is probable that church music was a little more colourful in performance than we are apt to believe. There are grounds for thinking that instruments were used to accompany the chant. Reed-pipes, trumpets, drums, bagpipes, and hurdy-gurdies all appear in illuminated manuscripts of the period, and there is no reason to suppose they were not actually used. The only difficulty is that these instruments were also used for ordinary entertainment and therefore had strong 'irreligious' associations, which would certainly have offended stricter churchmen.

One instrument whose use we can be absolutely sure of, however, is the organ.

There were at least three sizes of organ available at this time.

The small Portative Organ, which could be carried by the player and was therefore useful in processions. The rather larger Positive Organ, suitable for small churches. And the Great Organ, to be found in cathedrals.

A vivid description of the organ at Winchester (c 950) makes it quite clear that some of the larger organs were veritable monsters. The writer credits it with 400 pipes and 26 bellows, and claims that 70 men were needed to pump it, while 3 players presided at a keyboard consisting of heavy wooden sliders, which they pulled out to let the air whistle through the pipes. The sound was doubtless a noble one.

CHAPTER II

CHURCH MUSIC IN THE THIRTEENTH CENTURY

THE music of the twelfth and thirteenth centuries is generally known as the ARS ANTIQUA—a term wished upon it by musicians of the fourteenth century, who considered their own music to be an ARS NOVA: a new and, by implication, superior art.

This was an exciting period in European history. The great unifying power was still the Christian Church; and never more so than when Pope Urban II launched the First Crusade to recapture the Holy Land from the Turks in 1096. By a happy chance, the benefits of crusading turned out to be economic as well as spiritual. Wealth from the east began to flow back along the routes the crusaders took: first into the new commercial cities of Italy, and then on into northern Europe. It is no accident that the great architectural expression of the age—the Gothic cathedral—is not a church in a monastery, but a church in a city.

Gothic architecture, with its pointed arches and its capacity to soar to great heights (reaching out as it were to God in His Heaven) is the first flower of a distinctly Western style of building. The earlier, Romanesque, architecture owed much to the past. Its curved arches and heavy grandeur, and the very shape of its buildings were derived from ancient Rome and cannot express the new spirit. But the soaring, vertical lines of the Gothic cathedral are the work of a new kind of man, confident and proudly aware of himself.

Church music shares something of this new-found freedom. Though it remains closely involved with its heritage of plainchant, it is no longer rigidly shackled to it. And, for the first time, we begin to be aware of composers as individuals.

During this period France became the cultural leader of Europe, and Paris the focal point of all activity. A University was founded there in 1140, and in 1163 the first stones of Notre Dame were laid. It is with this great cathedral that the first important composers in the history of Western music are associated. They are: Léonin, and his successor Pérotin.

The actual dates of these two composers are not known, but they should be thought of as flourishing between about 1150 and 1230. Both were concerned with writing in the various styles of free organum.

Léonin's organa are two-part music. He used two main styles of composition. In the first, the plainsong melody is spun out in long notes, with the added part dancing above in a free and often complex manner. In the second, both voices keep the same rhythmic pattern. Both styles can be found in the same work—the one at moments when the plainsong is simple, and the other when it becomes florid.

Pérotin also composed organa—not only in two parts, but in three and four as well. The added parts are held together by being in the same rhythm. On occasion, they even exchange actual melodic shapes. Thus, three phrases that occur in one voice in the order *a b c*, might appear at the same time in another voice as *b c a*, and in a third as *c a b*. This kind of interchange lies at the root of contrapuntal imitation: a device that was to play a very large part in the development of music.

Contemporary accounts refer to Léonin as 'the best composer of organum', but Pérotin is called 'the best composer of discant'. By this they meant that Pérotin excelled in the composition of the CLAUSULA: a short section of lively, almost dance-like music which is inserted in the more stately progress of organum and was very probably played by instruments only. Pérotin is even thought to have added sections of this kind to the organa that Léonin composed.

Besides organa and clausulae, Pérotin wrote music in the style of the CONDUCTUS and the MOTET, both of which are the invention of this period.

In the conductus none of the parts are borrowed from plainchant. The entire piece is the work of the composer. All the parts, whether there are two, three, or four, move in more or less the same rhythm, and all use the same words. As the conductus was used to accompany the priest's progress about the church, this march-like uniformity was essential.

The motet, on the other hand, was a more complicated affair. It seems to have come into existence as a result of giving words to the instrumental clausulae that had been added to the organa, and then treating them as compositions in their own right.

The result was a piece of music that employed several sets of words. Thus, the lowest part (the TENOR, or 'holding part') used the words of the original organum. But the added parts introduced new texts: one, two, or three, according to the number of voices involved. By the end of the thirteenth century it was even possible to find two languages being used in the same composition: Latin, for the original plainchant, and the everyday language of the country for the added voices. In practice, however, the muddle may not have been quite so bad as it may seem, for the long notes of the plainchant were often played on an instrument.

Unlike the organa and clausulae, which were exclusively concerned with the liturgy, both the conductus and motet are to be found as secular works during this period. The musical style is the same, and only the words, praising worldly delights far removed from the joys of heaven, point the difference.

From the middle of the thirteenth century the motet was the style of composition most favoured by composers. It is therefore not surprising to find that this is the one form to be taken over wholeheartedly by the composers of the following century.

Besides the actual music they produced, which by any standards represents a high-water mark in creative invention, the composers of Notre Dame must be credited with new developments in musical notation.

While it was perfectly possible to show the relative heights of the notes, no one had yet hit upon a method of showing their different lengths and thus their rhythmic relationships. As music became more complicated, the need for this further information became more and more essential. To cope with the situation the Notre Dame composers began to make use of a system which we now call MODAL RHYTHM.

This involved arranging rhythms into a set of six basic patterns, which were probably derived from the poetic metres of ancient Greece. By writing his notes in conventional groups, called LIGATURES, the composer was able to show which rhythmic mode the music belonged to. The singers could then slip into the appropriate rhythm.

The system had its limitations, however. It allowed triple rhythms, and indeed was entirely based on them, but left no

Ve-ni Cre - a-tor_ Spi-ri - tus, Men-tes tu-o-rum vi - si - ta:

Im-ple_ su-per-na_gra-ti-a Quae tu cre-a-sti__pec-to-ra. A - men_

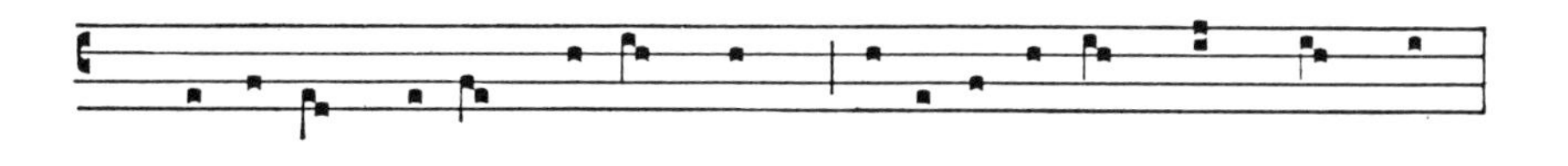

Gregorian Chant: Hymn *Veni Creator Spiritus*

The Office Hymn for the Second Vespers of Whitsunday, the words of which date, most probably, from the ninth century. The chant itself is older.

Come, O creator Spirit, come,
And make within our hearts thy home:
To us thy Grace celestial give,
Who of thy breathing move and live.

Parallel Organum: Sequence *Rex caeli, Domine*

The original plainsong is in the upper voice. The added *vox organalis* moves, for the most part, in parallel fourths below. This example comes from the ninth century treatise *Musica enchiriadis*.

1 King of the Heavens, Lord of the wave-sounding sea
2 Of the shining sun and of the squalid earth

Fauxbourdon

This anonymous instrumental extract dates from about the year 1300 and contains the parallel sixths and thirds typical of 'English descant'.

room for duple patterns. In other words: $\frac{3}{4}$ was possible, but not $\frac{2}{4}$.

The reasoning behind this is to be found in the general philosophical beliefs of the age, which held that the universe was governed by a kind of Divine arithmetic. The number 3 was regarded as an unassailable symbol of perfection—The Trinity, in fact. Armed with this belief, medieval man was forever trying to fit his thoughts into logical schemes that would mirror the greater logic of the universe.

As might be expected, composers did not follow their theories very closely when it came actually to composing music. They devised ways of avoiding what would otherwise have been a rather monotonous rum-ti-tum lilt. But, with all its faults, the new theory embodied a step worth taking.

CHAPTER III

SECULAR MUSIC: TWELFTH AND THIRTEENTH CENTURIES

IT would be quite wrong to suppose that the only worthwhile music composed during the period we have been considering was intended for use in church. The music of popular entertainment must have played an equal if not more important part in daily life, and it too had its glories.

Unfortunately none of the popular songs and dances written before the ninth century have survived, and precious few after that. Only the church musician felt the necessity of recording his thoughts, and he alone had the means to do so. The musician-in-the-street sang his songs and played his dances, and then trusted to his memory. Inevitably, much of his art was soon forgotten.

Until about the year 1100 music outside the church was in the hands of two kinds, or classes, of musician. First, there was the uneducated, lower-class JONGLEUR (Juggler); and then, the GOLIARD: the wandering scholar, the student-priest who had not yet taken vows.

The jongleurs must be thought of as performers and entertainers, rather than poets and composers. They played instruments and sang, but they also danced and juggled and performed tricks. They were, in short, a complete variety act. Each year during Lent, when forbidden to perform in public, they gathered together for a kind of refresher course to learn new songs and work out new tricks.

However much the ordinary man may have enjoyed their capers, the jongleurs found little favour either with the Church, or with civil authorities. In those stern eyes they were rogues and vagabonds, owing allegiance to no man and capable of every kind of scandalous behaviour. Gradually, however, they became more respectable—or were simply forced to mend their ways. They attached themselves to noble households, either as Musicians of War, playing trumpets and drums, or as Chamber Musicians, playing and singing for the general entertainment of their masters.

It seems likely that they borrowed most of their music, using either the folksongs and dances of the time, or even adapting such church music as came their way. So far as songs are concerned the jongleurs are mainly associated with the so-called CHANSON DE GESTE—a long recital of the exploits of some hero (real or imaginary), sung to a simple melodic phrase which is repeated over and over again. They probably accompanied their singing with an instrument (such as the harp), or played brief interludes on the fiddle, or hurdy-gurdy (vielle) to give the recital a little variety.

The general name for the kind of dances a jongleur might play is ESTAMPIE. Musically these consist of a number of paired phrases which employ, alternately, two kinds of ending: the open (ouvert) ending, and the closed (clos). These endings appear consistently in every pair of phrases, and so the effect of a rhyme is set up. Dances were very popular, and the Church often felt obliged to speak out against their corrupting influence.

Though educated and much more creative, the goliards were also frowned upon by authority. They wandered over Europe, more or less in pursuit of learning, composing and singing Latin songs on various subjects. Often these were extremely beautiful and filled with the most exquisite lyrical poetry. But they could also be humorous, bitterly satirical, and even downright obscene: and this, inevitably, brought down the wrath of the Church.

With the foundation of Universities (Paris and Bologna at the beginning of the twelfth century, and Oxford about a hundred years later) the goliards began to fade from the scene. There was no longer any reason to wander from one famous teacher to another, and once they had assumed settled habits their music-making ceased.

The most important secular music of the twelfth and thirteenth centuries is associated with the TROUBADOURS of southern France, and the TROUVERES of northern France. Both were composer-poets connected in some way with princely courts. Often they were men of rank and nobility; but even when they were of humble origin their art was distinguished by its aristocratic grace and chivalrous intent.

For the most part they sang of love—a disembodied, idealistic love, compounded of knightly vows and elegant despair. Taking a leaf out of the Church's book, which at this time tended to stress the worship of The Virgin Mary, they set woman on a pedestal and praised her from afar. They mirror exactly the high hopes and spirituality that inspired the first crusades.

Unlike the goliards, the troubadours and trouvères wrote their songs in the language of the country. Musically they were much more enterprising, and their songs can be divided into several distinct types, each with its own kind of formal shape. The most important of these song-forms: the ROTROUENGE, the LAI, the BALLADE, the VIRELAI, and the RONDEAUX, developed into the main types of secular music of the fourteenth and fifteenth centuries.

With the exception of the lai, which is very like the sequence in structure (see Chapter I), these song-forms all make use of the REFRAIN—a melodic phrase that returns several times, and which may very well have been sung by the audience. In its developed state, the rondeaux takes the device furthest: here the refrain occurs at the beginning, and at the end, and in the middle of each verse.

The names of many troubadours and trouvères have come down to us. They include, among the troubadours: Marcabru of Gascony, Bernart de Ventadorn, Guiraut de Riuier, and Bertran de Born. And trouvères: Blondel de Nesle, Thibaut (King of Navarre), and Adam de la Halle.

The influence of these courtly composer-poets can be seen particularly in Germany, where, during the twelfth and thirteenth centuries, a similar group arose, called MINNESINGERS—the 'singers of chivalrous love'. Their songs are like those of the troubadours and trouvères, but they lay much more emphasis on praise of The Virgin Mary as the ideal of all womanhood. Among the most famous of them were: Wolfram von Eschenbach, Neithart von Reuenthal, and Walther von der Vogelweide.

In Italy the influence was less obvious and seems to have been confined mainly to lyric poetry. Indeed, secular music developed comparatively late in this area, possibly because the Church was able to keep a much more effective eye on the dangers of mere entertainment. There is, however, a considerable body of LAUDI SPIRITUALI—hymns of praise sung by bands of penitents as they wandered about the countryside. When not singing, the penitents were liable to indulge in bouts of flagellation, the better to underline their despair at the sins and miseries of this world. In this way they expected to win forgiveness in the world to come.

In general terms, the entertainment music of this period differs from church music in that it is much more rhythmic and dance-like, and therefore apt to fall into repeated patterns. Its melodies are less confined and intense than plainsong, and contain certain hints of national characteristics. The words it uses, of course, are part of the everyday language of the country, and this fact alone would help to give the music a local flavour.

Songs were almost certainly sung to an accompaniment, played probably on a lute, or small harp. And for dance music there would have been bagpipes, the early fiddle, the hurdy-gurdy, reed pipes and recorders, and all manner of drums and bells. It needs little imagination to see that the effect must have been lively, colourful, and entertaining.

CHAPTER IV

THE ARS NOVA OF THE FOURTEENTH CENTURY

DURING the fourteenth century the religious certainties of the Middle Ages received a number of severe blows. For some time the Popes of Rome, not content merely to be the spiritual leaders of Christendom, had played an increasing and meddlesome part in European politics. By the year 1300, however, the kings of both France and England had rejected the idea that salvation lay in being subject to Rome, and in 1303 the French king took matters into his own hands, kidnapped the Pope and set him up at Avignon. For seventy-five years French Popes ruled by courtesy of the French monarchy.

But there was worse to come. Italy grew fretful at the slight, and in 1378 Europe was amazed to hear that there were now two Popes—one in Rome and one at Avignon—and both claimed absolute authority. This state of affairs lasted until 1418, and in the meantime the prestige of the Catholic Church rapidly dwindled.

The decline of spiritual leadership came at a crucial time in the history of Europe. A struggle for power between France and England—the birthpangs of two emerging nations—resulted in The Hundred Year's War (1337-1453). In 1349 the Great Plague of the Black Death carried off nearly 25 million people, heavily underlining the apparent futility of human existence. Thus, at a time when the Church should have been a hope, a comfort, and an inspiration, it was found wanting.

Small wonder, then, that the composers of the fourteenth century began to find greater satisfaction in writing for the courts of the aristocracy. They still composed for the Church, of course, and most of them held minor religious orders, but the important advances fell largely in the field of secular music.

To the musical theorists of the time this was nevertheless a period of hope and innovation. Theirs, they felt, was a new art, superior to everything that had gone before. And, borrowing from the title of a treatise by the poet, composer and theorist Philippe de Vitry (1291-1361), they hailed the dawn of an ARS NOVA.

What de Vitry set forth was simply a new method of notation, which he illustrated in his own motets. The precise details need not concern us: it is enough to say that he introduced new symbols and used them to place duple and triple time on an equal footing. He thus gave to French music the possibility of a much freer kind of rhythm, which no longer had to lean on the artificial convention of the rhythmic modes.

So far as the actual music of the period is concerned, the honours are evenly divided between France and Italy. The developments that took place can best be seen in the individual contributions of two composers: Guillaume de Machaut (c 1300-c 1377) in France, and Francesco Landini (c 1325-c 1397) in Italy.

In spite of being in Holy Orders, Machaut passed most of his life as a servant of the nobility, and in consequence seems to have composed rather more music for entertainment than for use in church. Of the 140 pieces that have been preserved (a large number for those days, and a striking testimony to the esteem in which he was held) only 7 are liturgical (6 motets and a mass). The remainder consists of ballades, virelais, rondeaux, lais, and secular motets.

Machaut's liturgical music shares the rhythmic preoccupations of the age. His motets make use of a new structural device, which may have been invented by Philippe de Vitry, and which is now known as ISORHYTHM—that is: 'the same rhythm'.

The ISORHYTHMIC MOTET came into existence during the first quarter of the thirteenth century and served as the basic 'classical' form for the next hundred years. During that time it appeared in the music of France, Burgundy, England, and Italy. The idea is simple: the plainsong tenor, which forms the backbone of the motet, is divided into sections. Each section is given the same rhythm. It is then strung throughout the motet (sometimes with breaks in between the different sections), and, if necessary, repeated.

This rhythmic pattern is known as the TALEA. It must not be confused with a melody (known to the theorists of the day as a COLOR): it is a rhythm and nothing more. The fact that the rhythmic pattern is repeated, regardless of the melodic shape, gives the music a feeling of unity.

That, at least, was the theory. In practice it must be admitted that, as a structural device, isorhythm is rather more effective on paper than it is to the casual listening ear.

Isorhythm soon came to be applied to all the voices of the motet. But it is important to realise that each voice kept to its own kind of melodic shape and its own rhythmic pattern. There were, as yet, no shared ideas crossing from one voice to another.

Machaut's purely secular music, on the other hand, is very much an echo of the past. It has something of the courtly spirit of the trouvères. The ballades are the most interesting and individual of his entertainment pieces. They consist of a vocal line (or duet) accompanied by one or two instruments. They are quite freely invented and borrow nothing from plainsong. In listening to them it is easy to understand his claim that all his music was 'deeply felt'.

There is one further technical feature in the music of this period which deserves special attention. This is the device known as CANON—the idea of one voice imitating another exactly, like a well-disciplined echo.

In France the form that exploited canon was called the CHACE. As its name suggests, it was a vocal composition with words about hunting—the voices literally 'chasing' each other hither and thither. We shall meet the same device in Italian music.

Though Paris was still the artistic and intellectual centre of Europe, the fourteenth century shows increasingly a tendency on the part of certain northern Italian cities to assert their own artistic independence. The general history of Italy is worth considering for a moment. Throughout the medieval period the most travelled trade routes with the East went through the cities of northern and central Italy. As trading posts they flourished and grew rich. Inevitably, communities of this potential fell under the guiding hands of certain strong and gifted families:

the Sforzas of Milan, the Gonzagas of Mantua, the Malatestas of Rimini, the Medici of Florence, and so on.

Once firmly established, these families began to vie with each other in the magnificence of their outward show. Soon they began to encourage art. Thus it was that by the fourteenth century many schools of composers flourished throughout the country. Even though their music lay, in the main, heavily under the influence of France, the glimmerings of an independent style can be observed. That independence is summed up in the interest they took in melody—an aspect of music that the French had tended to neglect in favour of rhythmic ingenuity.

The new form that embodied this essentially Italian point of view was the MADRIGAL. This was a two-part composition, the upper voice being considerably more florid than the lower (which might well be played by an instrument). Most madrigals consist of three verses of three lines each, and a final verse of two lines. This final verse is called the RITORNELLO. The three-line verses repeat the same melody, but the ritornello breaks new ground.

As music these compositions are sweet and melodious and immensely singable. They have a warmth and good humour that sets them apart from the more intellectual genius of France. And they make use of one technical feature that was to have enormous importance in the development of music: IMITATION.

Imitation occurs when one voice repeats at least a part of what another voice has just sung. Any composition that uses this device is bound to hold together in a way that is as satisfying to the ear as it is on paper. Melodic shapes are tossed from one voice to another, so that the entire piece can be heard to evolve from the same material.

A similar device, as we have already seen, is the canon (though here, of course, the imitation is strict and continuous), and this, in Italy, is to be found in the CACCIA. Like the French chace these are hunting songs; and like the madrigal they consist of a main verse (one only) and a ritornello. They are usually three-part compositions, with the two upper voices chasing each other in canon, while the lowest remains free (and may have been performed on an instrument).

This tendency to bind all the voices together by means of imitation is a foretaste of the way in which the music of the fifteenth and sixteenth centuries was to go. It stands in direct opposition to the ars nova style of France, which emphasised the independence of each melodic part.

It is not hard to see, in this choice of styles, that France was still a very Gothic-minded country, favouring the untrammeled spirituality of floating melodic lines. While Italy, on the other hand, looked forward to the human warmth of the Renaissance and opted for an altogether more worldly kind of music.

The difference can also be seen in the literature of the two countries. The typical French poet is Froissart (c 1333-1404), whose work could find room for long chivalric poems that hark back to the Chanson de Geste. The typical Italian writers, however, are still read for their down-to-earth humanity: Dante (1265-1321), Petrarch (1304-1374), and Boccaccio (1313-1375). A comparison between the intense spirituality of French Gothic architecture (the cathedral at Amiens, for example) with Giotto's campanile in Florence, lends further point to the difference of attitude.

English genius, in the person of Geoffrey Chaucer (c 1340-1400), would seem to be inclined more to the humanism of Italy than the idealism of France.

Just as Machaut sums up the achievement of the ars nova in France, so also Francesco Landini sums up the glories of the Italian style. Though organist of the church of San Lorenzo, in Florence, he left no church music. His fame rests entirely upon his madrigals, caccie, and BALLATE.

The ballata corresponds to the French virelai—that is to say: it consists of several verses, each of which begins and ends with a refrain. Landini's ballate are for two and three voices.

Despite Pope John XXII, who issued a Bull in 1324-25 denouncing the wanton lasciviousness of the 'new music', the fourteenth century appears as a time when secular compositions began to creep ahead of music intended for use in the church. And it is this tendency that became increasingly a part of the European musical scene in the years that followed.

NOTES

NOTES

NOTES

NOTES

PART TWO

The Renaissance 1400-1600

CHAPTER V

CHURCH MUSIC IN THE FIFTEENTH CENTURY

MAN's attitude to the world around him underwent fundamental changes during the fifteenth century. In the year 1400 the spirit of the times was still that of the medieval world, even though religious confidence had already been crudely challenged by the outrageous paradox of the Great Schism. By 1500 a new spirit was abroad—a spirit based not upon the idea that this world was merely a proving-ground for the soul and a prelude to the ultimate realities of heaven, but upon the realisation that man had a dignity of his own, and that the world was worth exploring and enjoying for its own sake. To the medieval mind man had been little more than a cog in the Divine machinery that governed the universe. In the period we now call the Renaissance he became the focal point of human interest.

Translated into musical terms, this change of attitude brought about an increasing interest in secular music. And though church music remained the over-riding preoccupation, composers can be seen making their contributions with a much freer hand and with much less regard for the traditional sanctity of plainchant. The secular spirit was widespread.

In terms of leadership the European musical scene began the fifteenth century under the influence of English composers. But the pattern soon changed, and from about 1430 it was the Burgundian-Flemish composers who set the pace. Italy, in contrast to the astonishing upsurge of her painters and architects, had little to offer.

The most important names in the first half of the century are: the Englishman John Dunstable (c 1370-1453), and the Burgundians Gilles Binchois (1400-1460) and Guillaume Dufay (c 1400-1474).

Dunstable's influence was strong in France—doubtless because, as musician to John, Duke of Bedford, who was Regent of France from 1422 to 1435, he spent much time there. French composers were quick to copy the English style, which contained many novel features.

Chief among them was the English delight in sonority. Instead of the usual kind of organum in parallel fifths and octaves, they employed thirds and sixths—which, of course, sound much sweeter. This device is known as FAUXBOURDON.

There is also in English music a much greater feeling for chord progression—the composers seem more aware of harmony for its own sake. This, coupled with their interest in a very lyrical kind of vocal writing and their tendency to give all the voices music of equal importance, proved very attractive to the continental masters. Their music, as a result, began to disclose a new freshness and liveliness.

Another important feature borrowed from English practice is the free way in which plainchant now came to be treated. Dunstable and his contemporaries cheerfully added new notes and omitted others. They changed the pitch of phrases according to their needs, and instead of keeping the chant in the tenor they were quite happy to let it wander from voice to voice. Furthermore, they took to ornamenting the chant and making variations upon it—a practice known as PARAPHRASING.

A further innovation is to be found in their use of the plainchant to give a sense of unity to the mass. Often, they based each movement on the same chant. A mass constructed in this way is called a CANTUS FIRMUS MASS: the chant is the cantus firmus, or 'fixed voice'.

Far from being wedded to plainchant as a basis for their religious music, English composers were also prepared to write absolutely new music. Nearly half of Dunstable's motets and mass movements make no kind of reference to plainchant whatsoever—a remarkable state of affairs when you consider the veneration in which it had so far been held.

Altogether the English approach to composition was both lively and inventive, and therefore extremely influential.

The importance of the Burgundian composers stems largely from political accident. During the Hundred Years War whole areas of France came under English rule—indeed, after his victory at Agincourt Henry V styled himself King of England and France. In subduing the French, however, Henry had received help from the Dukes of Burgundy, and even though the English withdrew after 1435 this dukedom contrived to remain powerful. Its territories at this time included most of central and southern France, north and south Holland, Friesland, Zeeland, and what is now Belgium.

Both Duke Philip (the Good) and his successor Charles (the Bold) were passionately devoted to music. At their magnificent court at Dijon they maintained a splendid band of singers and composers, in imitation of the Papal Court at Rome. Nearly all the important composers of the century were connected in some way with Burgundy. Binchois, Busnois, and Dufay worked at the court, and Ockeghem and Josquin des Prés were natives of its northern territories.

Dufay and Binchois, and their contemporaries, borrowed not only from English composers (as we have seen), but also from the example of late thirteenth century Italy. In particular they began to employ melodic imitation between the different voices, in a way that is reminiscent of the Italian caccia (see Chapter IV).

Their own inventions include a new method of giving unity to the mass. They placed a 'head motive' (a recognisable melodic fragment) at the beginning of each section, usually in the highest voice where it could be heard clearly.

Equally at home with sacred and secular music, Dufay and Binchois both show clear evidence of their remarkable genius in the CHANSON that form so large a part of their output. At this date the term chanson is a general one, covering all French secular composition. The most usual form, however, is the rondeaux, which had now displaced the ballade in popularity (see Chapters III and IV).

The important composers of the second half of the century belong to what is usually called the Flemish School, though it is reasonable to think of them as sharing the traditions established by the Burgundian court. They include: Johannes Ockeghem (c 1420-c 1495), Antoine Busnois (d 1492), Jacob Obrecht (1450-1505), Heinrich Isaac (c 1450-1517), and, greatest of all, Josquin des Prés (c 1450-1521).

Their main contribution consists of polyphonic settings of the mass, liturgical motets, and, in the secular field, chanson. What they achieved in these forms is of the utmost importance, simply because it became the basis of the culminating phase of polyphonic art: the glories of the sixteenth century.

From Ockeghem onwards composers began to exploit four-part textures, adding the lower register of the bass voice both in sacred and secular works. They began also to contrast passages of imitative counterpoint with passages in a simpler, chordal style.

In general, their counterpoint grew more and more ingenious

and fluent. Besides the devices of canon and imitation, which we have already noted, they began to introduce AUGMENTATION (stretching out a melody in longer notes), INVERSION (turning a melody upside down), and RETROGRADATION (playing backwards). This latter device gave rise to the CANON CANCRIZANS (Crab Canon), in which the imitating voice plays its theme from Z to A, as it were, instead of the normal A to Z.

To this we must add an increasing tendency to make all the melodic parts equally interesting. And, by skilfully overlapping the parts (ie by making one voice begin a new phrase before the other voices have finished with theirs) a move towards producing the kind of texture that flows on throughout each movement without any obvious breaks.

In spite of their obvious technical ingenuity, the Flemish composers must not be thought of as merely clever. Their music is both powerful and beautiful, and they used their skills with discretion and artistry.

Listening to their works we may notice that these composers had become aware of the role that harmony can play in giving to music a sense of movement. Certain combinations of notes, concords, sound relaxed and pleasant. Other combinations, the discords, have the opposite effect: they sound ugly, restless and incomplete. If our ears are made unhappy by the sound of a discord, they can be made happy again if that discord gives way to a concord. In other words: our ears have longed to hear the discord *move* into the concord. Composers began to realise this fact, and thus by creating discords and then letting them glide into the appropriate concord they were able to give their music the appearance of moving forward.

The device the fifteenth century established for exploiting this effect is known as a SUSPENSION. It consists of three steps: the 'preparation', in which all the notes are concordant with one another; the suspension itself, in which one note is held in its original position while the others move on to a new chord; and finally the 'resolution', in which the 'suspended' note now falls into its rightful place in the new chord, and therefore ceases to have a discordant effect.

During this period the methods of holding the movements of the mass together remained basically what they had been during the first half of the century. Isorhythmic techniques were still in use, and so was the cantus firmus method. In the Cantus Firmus Mass the borrowed melody was presented either in its natural state or in a paraphrased form, and it was now quite as common for it to be a secular tune as an actual chant. One of the most famous and frequently employed tunes of the time is the French chanson *L'homme armé*. Few composers seem to have been able to resist taking it as a basis for their compositions.

It is important to realise that the practice of basing a work firmly upon old material does not in any sense imply a lack of creative power in the composers of the period. This was their way of paying homage to a tradition they respected, and their creativity is to be seen in the use to which they put their borrowings.

One of the most extreme kinds of borrowing can be seen in the so-called PARODY MASS. Here the composer took over not just one, but all the voice parts of some previously composed piece, either quoting it directly, or blending it in with his own new ideas. Often the quotation is so drastically re-worked that it is hard to recognise the original. Again, it was what the composer did with the borrowed material that mattered, and not the fact that he had borrowed.

Without any doubt the fifteenth century is a high-water mark in the history of music. Out of it came works that can still stir the imagination with their beauty and impress the intellect with their skill. The flower of this great creative upsurge, Josquin des Prés, was recognised in his own day as a supreme master. He stands today as one of the great composers of all time.

CHAPTER VI

FIFTEENTH CENTURY SECULAR MUSIC

ALTHOUGH very little entertainment music of the period has survived, there is ample proof that it played an important part in daily life. Fifteenth century paintings show groups of minstrels performing on a variety of instruments. Account-books tell us how many minstrels the courts employed, and roughly what their duties were. Chroniclers remind us that music played its part in the pageantry of military life. In addition to the serious music of the Church, then, we have every reason to suppose that a lighter, utility kind of music was in common use.

There were two distinct types of minstrel: Chamber Minstrels, and Minstrels of War. Apart from the obvious duty of giving signals on the field of battle, the latter ministered in time of peace to the general pomp and ceremony of court life. Trumpet fanfares would herald the arrival of a nobleman on some important occasion. The more exalted the man, the greater the musical tumult was likely to be.

Domestic musicians were also employed in great numbers. They provided music for all occasions: dances, songs, music for feasts, and so on. Few of them were composers in their own right, but they were expert in the art of improvisation and carried in their heads a large repertory of popular tunes. The instruments they played include: recorders, oboes (shawms), trumpets, trombones (sackbuts), harps, lutes, strings (viols), small organs (the regal, for example), and the earliest stringed keyboard instrument: the clavichord.

One of the most important kinds of dance from this period is the French BASSE DANSE. A favourite combination of instruments in performing it was a sackbut and two shawms. The shawms improvised melodies above the sackbut, which confined itself to one or other of the traditional basse-danse tunes—rather in the way that religious music was built round a chant. Many of these bass themes were borrowed from popular chansons. They were always played in long notes, however, and therefore lose their rhythmic identity.

The Italian BALLO, on the other hand, made use of borrowed tunes but kept them in their original rhythms. It seems probable that the ballo was sung and danced at the same time.

By the end of the century the types of available dance had greatly multiplied—much to the disgust of church men. Many of them bore strong national characteristics: particular rhythms, and turns of phrase. It became the custom to pair the dances for contrast—a quick dance followed by a slow dance, or vice versa. This practice led, as we shall see, to the creation of the instrumental suite.

Next to the French chanson, the most popular kinds of fifteenth century song were the German LIED, the English CAROL, and the Italian FROTTOLA.

Like the chanson, the German lied is a polyphonic song, usually for three voices. But there is an important difference in its manner of construction: whereas the tune of the chanson was given to the highest voice, even when the whole piece was built round a borrowed tenor, the principal melody of the lied was always placed in the tenor—the lowest voice in a three-part composition. In this respect the lied was rather old-fashioned. Among its composers we may note: Heinrich Finck (c 1445-1527) and Thomas Stolzer (c 1470-1526); and among the great manuscript collections of lieder, the three song books of Locheim, Glogau, and Schedel, all dating from the middle of the century.

The English carol, also a polyphonic song, was not restricted to Christmas events for its subject matter. Hymns to The Virgin Mary, prayers to particular saints, thanksgiving songs for victory (the famous *Agincourt Song*, for example), are all carols. The common factor is not their subject matter, but their musical structure. This consists of a BURDEN and a VERSE. The burden appears at the beginning of the carol and then after each verse. The verses themselves sometimes end with the same refrain.

Although by no means as elaborate as their continental counterparts, these English secular songs are often very beautiful —both as music and as poetry. It seems likely that they were sung in connection with various ceremonies: processions at Christmas time, feasts, civic receptions, and so forth.

The Italian frottola belongs rather more to the sixteenth century, but its beginnings in the carnival songs of Florence may be noted at this point. As can be imagined from its origins, the frottola was altogether simpler and more popular in style than the polyphonic lied and chanson. Its tunes are usually square-cut and straightforward, and the parts much more like accompanying harmonies than independent melodies in their own right. Among the composers of frottola are a number of Flemish masters who visited Italy: Josquin des Prés and Heinrich Isaac in particular. Indeed, one of the remarkable things about the Italian scene is the absence of great musical figures who were actually native to the country. It would seem that the spirit of the Renaissance, that had flowered in Italy through the genius of its painters (Fra Angelico, Uccello, Botticelli, Leonardo da Vinci, Raphael, Bellini, Montegna, Giorgione, Carpaccio, and a dozen more), its sculptors (Donatello, Ghiberti, Michelangelo), and its architects (Brunelleschi, Michelozzi, Alberti, Bramante), had yet to find a way of expressing itself in terms of music.

Part-songs, however, were not the only kind of secular songs that flourished in the fifteenth century. There were also solo songs, and the largest body of these is associated with the German MASTERSINGERS.

Although they regarded themselves as heirs to the subtle art of the Minnesingers (see Chapter III), the Mastersingers were in fact ordinary tradesmen who met in their spare time and sang. Their meetings soon grew into organised Guilds (very much a feature of the rising middle-class tradesman at this period), and, characteristically, they set up rules and regulations governing the admission of new recruits.

To be a 'master' singer you were obliged to compose both the words and music of at least one song—keeping, of course, a careful eye on the pedantic 'rules of invention' that other masters had built up. Though much exercised by the rules, even the most famous of the late Mastersingers, Hans Sachs (1494-1576), was seldom actually visited by inspiration. But the importance of the movement in creating a love of music throughout middle-class Germany cannot be overestimated.

One small sign of the particular fields in which German musical genius was later to flower can be seen in the collections of organ music that were made in the fifteenth century. The earliest of these, the *Buxheimer Orgelbuch*, contains two pieces of Conrad Paumann (c 1410-1473), an organist whose virtuosity was acclaimed throughout Europe. In the second half of the century several more organ virtuosi came into prominence: Arnolt Schlick, Paul Hofhaimer, and Hans Buchner, for example. These men represent the beginnings of a new class of musician, neither minstrel nor learned church-musician, but a specialist in the art of playing a particular instrument and in writing music to suit its peculiar needs.

Most German organ music at this time, however, is not instrumental in the strict sense. It is vocal music, transferred to the keyboard and tricked out with a few ornamental flourishes. The only surviving examples of a really characteristic keyboard style are to be found in a handful of virginal pieces by the Englishman Hugh Aston (c 1480-1522), and far in advance of the time.

CHAPTER VII

SIXTEENTH CENTURY POLYPHONY

DESPITE its dazzling achievements, the sixteenth century must be regarded as essentially a period of artistic cross-currents and contradictions. In the foreground we see the brilliant flowering of vocal polyphony, at the hands of such masters as Roland de Lassus, Palestrina, William Byrd, Thomas Tallis, and Victoria. Behind, tentative and uncertain, but gaining confidence as the century wore on, are the principles and practices that were to dominate the 'new' music of the generations that followed.

Political and spiritual events were equally varied and contradictory. Spain, made wealthy by the colonial enterprise of the Conquistadors in the Americas, was now a power to be reckoned with. England, somewhat isolated from the immediate problems of Europe, was fast building herself up into a powerful nation. France remained strong and confident; while Germany and Italy were still divided into separate and comparatively weak states. The Holy Roman Empire, consisting now of Austria, the German States, north Italy, and Spain (an idea, rather than a territorial whole), was dominated by the Hapsburg rulers of Austria and Spain, even though it looked to Rome for spiritual guidance. Throughout Europe territorial squabbles alternated with religious strife. The whole period is therefore one of constantly changing patterns.

The dominating spirit of the age was that of HUMANISM—the exploration of man and the world around him. The growing concern with the practical possibilities of this world, as opposed to the theoretical promise of the next, had played its part in the previous century: now it became the driving force of all intellectual inquiry. In architecture this spirit sprang forth in the work of Michelangelo, Bramante, and Bernini. In painting we see it in Holbein, Breugel, Titian, Tintoretto, Veronese, Caravaggio, El Greco, and a host of other masters. In literature: Shakespeare, Marlowe, and Ben Jonson; Rabelais, Montaigne, and Ronsard; Cervantes, and Lope de Vega; Tasso, Ariosto, and Machiavelli. In science: Copernicus, Kepler, Ticho da Brahe, Galileo, and Bruno. In medicine: Paracelsus, Fallopius, Vesalius, and Paré. In exploration: Columbus, Vasco da Gama, Magellan, John and Sebastian Cabot, Drake, Cortez, and Pisarro. It was an age of wonders: the whole of civilised Europe bursting with the spirit of adventure and inquiry.

Though the achievements of sixteenth century music are spread impartially throughout Europe (there is scarcely a nation that did not make some contribution), the Renaissance musician looked to Italy as the source of his inspiration. The century may have begun with the domination of Flemish-born musicians, but it was the Italian spirit, subtly working upon the foundations the Netherlanders had left behind, that created the final all-powerful international style of the age.

The basis of this style is a smooth-flowing texture, woven from imitative motifs which pass effortlessly from one voice to another. When one 'point of imitation' is nearly exhausted, it begins to be replaced by a new motif—and so on, in a continuously evolving, seamless tapestry. It is a style that also takes account of the expressive character of harmonies, and the contrasting sonorities to be obtained from the varied combination and spacing of voices. In no sense does the virtuoso technique obscure or overwhelm the sheer beauty and emotional impact of the sound. Delightful and satisfying to perform, it is also music that addresses itself without reserve to the listener.

During this century the forms of Catholic church music remained the mass and the motet. Little by little, the cantus firmus type of mass dropped out of fashion. It was replaced by the various types of paraphrase mass (based on plainsong, or secular tunes), the parody mass (based on existing polyphonic material, such as a motet), and the freely-composed mass, constructed from entirely new material.

In varying degrees of intensity, this was the style and these were the forms shared by the great Catholic composers of the sixteenth century. Whether they were Flemish by birth and held important posts in other countries: Roland de Lassus (c 1532-1594), and Philippe de Monte (c 1521-1603), for example; Italians working for the Papal court: Giovanni Pierluigi da Palestrina (c 1525-1594); Englishmen: Thomas Tallis (c 1505-1585), and William Byrd (1543-1623); or Spaniards: Cristobal Morales (c 1500-1553), and Tomas Ludovico da Victoria (c 1540-1611); it was a style that all could share, and through it glorify the tenets of a great and powerful religion.

Only in Venice was there any obvious difference in the church music of the time. Here, at St Mark's, under the guidance of Adrian Willaert (c 1500-1562), Andrea Gabrieli (c 1520-1586), and his nephew Giovanni Gabrieli (1557-1612), music of peculiar magnificence was developed, involving techniques that were to have a considerable influence on the music of later composers.

The physical structure of St Mark's, with its double galleries, each complete with organ, prompted an elaborate grouping of choirs and instruments. Choirs of different ranges were made to contrast with each other, their music echoing about the building as it passed from one group to another. Similar antiphonal effects were obtained by using instruments (strings, brass, and organ), both by themselves and in combination with voices. The result of this cunning exploitation of space was sumptuous and very much in keeping with the ceremonial splendour of all Venetian art.

At its height, Catholic church music reflected the Renaissance love of magnificence. God might indeed be glorified in the ritual, but Renaissance man saw no reason why His Representatives on Earth should not share the glory. Religious ritual borrowed heavily from royal ceremonial. The Pope held court like any King, and the sumptuous polyphony that accompanied his celebration of High Mass reflected the magnificence of his office. Men went to church as much for musical pleasure as for prayer.

The delights of Catholic ritual were not to everybody's taste, however. In many eyes they were simply a sign that religion had lost its way. Moreover, the scandal of the Great Schism had been followed by a period of religious orthodoxy, accompanied by outbreaks of violence in which the Church persecuted those who did not agree with her views. By the beginning of the sixteenth century many men felt that it was possible to establish a relationship with God without the mediation of the Catholic Church.

Revolt came in 1517 when Martin Luther spoke out against the sale of indulgences—that is: the sale of pardon for committed sins. In due course he was excommunicated by the Pope, but his defiance continued. Lutheranism swept through Germany, and by 1526 the German princes had declared that its adherents should be allowed to preach and worship undisturbed. Intense pressure from Rome naturally followed. In 1529 the order was revoked, but this led a number of princes to protest—hence the term Protestant as a convenient label for all Reformed Churches. By 1555, however, the Lutherans had won their point and thereafter existed side by side with the Church of Rome in full religious equality. The revolt spread to Switzerland, under the leadership of Zwingli and Calvin; to France, with the Huguenots; and to England, in the form of the Anglican Church. In every case, the changes led to important musical developments.

Martin Luther, himself a competent musician, was convinced of the need for music in church services. He believed, however, that it should be brought closer to the ordinary worshipper. Therefore, while retaining much of the Catholic service (the mass and the motet, for example), he suggested that it should be sung in German rather than Latin. He encouraged also the use of new songs written in a simplified polyphony, which the congregation could take part in singing.

This concern to bring the congregation into direct contact with every possible aspect of the church service led eventually to the creation of a great body of religious song, called CHORALE, which was to prove as important to the development of German music as plainsong had been to Catholic polyphony.

Although Luther himself composed a number of chorales, the composer most concerned with their development was Johann Walther (1496-1570), whose *Geystliche Gesangk Buchleyn*, published in 1524, is the first of a long line of Protestant hymn books.

Chorale melody differs considerably in style from plainsong. It is governed by a definite metre, and moves in clear-cut, regular phrases, to a slow, even rhythm. More often than not, it uses major and minor keys. And because of its general simplicity it can be learned easily, even by musically uneducated congregations. In many instances chorales were simply modified versions of plainsong melodies, or adaptations of well-known tunes. Some of course, like Luther's *Ein' feste Burg*, were specially composed.

In France the Huguenot movement gave rise to a similar body of religious music. Psalms were translated in verse form and then set to music by such composers as Claude Goudimel (c 1505-1572), Claude Lejeune (1528-1600), and Jacques Mauduit (1557-1627). Their musical style includes passages of free polyphony as well as the more usual four-part chordal harmonisation. A similar treatment is to be found in the music, organised by Louis Bourgeois (c 1501-1561), of Calvin's *Genevan Psalter*.

The Anglican Church, unlike the Calvinists and Huguenots, retained the general structure of Catholic liturgy. It abandoned the use of Latin, however. The mass gave way to the Anglican Service: consisting of Morning Prayer and Evening Prayer, adapted from the old Canonical Hours, and the Communion Service, adapted from the mass itself. Motets gave way to the ANTHEM. An additional feature is the practice of singing psalms and canticles to simple metrical tunes harmonised in four parts.

To English composers the challenge of finding a way of setting their native language to music proved to be a stepping stone to great achievements. The work of Thomas Tallis, William Byrd, Christopher Tye, Thomas Weelkes, Thomas Tomkins, and Orlando Gibbons, will stand comparison with anything their continental contemporaries could produce.

The success of the Reformed Churches was a matter of great concern to Catholicism and prompted it to set its own house in order. Leading Catholics met, during the seven years between 1545 and 1563, to defend, clarify, and reform their traditional doctrines. Their sessions, The Council of Trent, touched also upon the position of music.

It was decided that music's main function was to promote a greater sense of worship in the congregation. From this it followed that the style of composition must allow the words to be heard clearly, that no secular material ought to be included

Isorhythm: Motet *Veni Sancte Spiritus* by John Dunstable
In this motet the technique of isorhythm is applied mainly to the 'tenor' cantus firmus (based on plainsong), which keeps to the same rhythmic pattern it had on its first appearance. Our illustration, however, shows the same principle applied to the other voices. The rhythms of bars 16 to 20 are almost identical with those in bars 1 to 5, though the tunes are quite different.

Sixteenth century polyphony: Madrigal *O che splendor* by Palestrina
An example of smooth-flowing, imitative polyphony.

Sixteenth century polyphony: *Stabat Mater* by Palestrina
An example of the simpler, one-note-for-each-syllable style, recommended by the Council of Trent.

in the fabric of the music, and that only the organ should be used to accompany the voices, or play solos.

At the Papal Chapel itself, the austere, compelling genius of Palestrina saw to it that the reforms were heeded. He made them the foundation of a great and noble style.

Elsewhere the Council's recommendations were not so well observed. There was, however, a general gain in the closer attention to word-setting that followed. And in this respect, church music was able to learn much from the secular styles of madrigal and chanson. Elaborate melismatic writing gave way to a more syllabic style. This in turn led to a texture that sounds less purely contrapuntal than earlier music. With these tendencies, as with the antiphonal effects of Venetian church music, we are on the threshold of a new musical art: the Baroque.

CHAPTER VIII

SECULAR MUSIC IN THE SIXTEENTH CENTURY

ALTHOUGH the importance of secular music increased considerably during the sixteenth century, composers still looked to the Church for their basic training. They began their careers as choirboys. If they showed talent they were taught to play instruments. Only after they had proved their skill as practical musicians would they be initiated into the mysteries of composition.

Once trained they might hope for a post in the choir of some cathedral or large church, or preferably, since it offered a much wider range of music-making, in the private chapel of a nobleman. Talented musicians were much sought after by the nobility, who offered them appropriate rewards. Besides their chapel duties they were expected to provide music for entertainment. And since the nobility considered an active interest in all the arts to be a sign of good breeding, there grew up the kind of atmosphere in which both music and musician could prosper.

In Italy the art of music was much helped by the rapid spread of ACADEMIES—societies founded for the advancement of science, literature, and the fine arts. Poets, musicians, artists, scientists, and enthusiastic amateurs would hold regular meetings to discuss and compare their studies. Concerts were given, in which gifted amateurs would join with professionals.

Nor was the cultivation of music confined to the upper classes. It spread also to the middle classes, who sang and played instruments with as much skill and pleasure as their betters. The corporations of large towns and cities also thought it essential to maintain groups of instrumentalists for civic functions. In Italy the city bands were composed of wind instruments, trumpets and trombones. Similar bands existed in Germany and England (the *Stadpfeiffer* and the *Waits*), but these included string players. And in villages everywhere the countryfolk had their own songs and dances—by no means despised by the more sophisticated members of society.

In as thoroughly musical an atmosphere as this, it is not surprising that secular music began to flourish.

The main developments took place in vocal music. Two important new forms emerged during the period: the CHANSON and the MADRIGAL. Though the chanson is associated mainly with France and the madrigal with Italy, both reflect a fruitful exchange of ideas between the two countries and underline once more the increasingly international character of sixteenth century art.

The French chanson owed much of its inspiration to the rise of a more simple and expressive style of lyric poetry among such writers as Ronsard and Marot. Taking a hint from the way in which the Italians composed their frottola (lively rhythms, a straightforward chordal style, and words set more or less syllabically), French composers began to set the new lyrics to music.

Important in this field are Claudin de Sermisy (c 1490-1562) and Clément Jannequin (c 1475-c 1560), who, though they wrote much religious music, were most admired for their chansons. The essence of these new works is their simplicity, and consequent suitability for amateur performance. They rely on brisk rhythms, simple melodies, and a realistic, often witty treatment of the text. The repetition of verses is one of their distinguishing features, as is the tendency for the words to tell or story or paint a picture. Jannequin's PROGRAMME CHANSONS are particularly interesting in this respect. Their titles alone are sufficient to suggest their general characteristics: *The Battle, The Hunt, The Song of the Birds,* for example.

The sixteenth century chanson is therefore quite different from the chanson of the previous century (see Chapter V). In its later stages it is represented by the work of Guillaume Costeley (c 1531-1606), Claude Goudimel (c 1505-1572), and Claude Lejeune (1525-1600).

Flemish composers, however, remained true to the polyphonic style of the earlier chanson. Consequently their work shows a more frequent use of imitation, and other contrapuntal techniques. In this respect they are direct successors to Josquin des Prés. The most important names are: Nicholas Gombert (c 1480-1556), Adrian Willaert (c 1500-1562), Jacon Arcadelt (c 1504-1567), and Roland de Lassus (c 1532-1594) (whose name, by the way, also appears in a Latinized form as Orlandus Lassus, and in Italian as Orlando di Lasso).

Like the French chanson, the Italian madrigal was sparked off by the literary developments. In its poetic form the madrigal consisted of a single stanza of no fixed length or rhyme-scheme, but containing either seven, or eleven syllables in each line. The musical equivalent, which began to develop around 1530 and has nothing in common with the Ars Nova madrigal (see Chapter IV), gradually evolved distinctive features, designed to express in detail the meaning of the poem. Imitation was all-important: new 'points' being introduced for each new thought in the poem, so that the music unrolled in a continuous progression. This kind of technique is obviously much more learned than that of the French chanson, where verse after verse was simply repeated to the same music.

The lead in developing the early madrigal was taken by the many Flemish-born composers working in Italy. Willaert, Arcadelt, and Philippe Verdelot (d.c 1567) were all active in the first half of the century. In its mature development, when it became rather more contrapuntal and introduced techniques for expressing emotions, and dramatic and pictorial ideas, the madrigal was mainly in the hands of the Italians. Andrea and Giovanni Gabrieli, Luca Marenzio (1553-1599), Carlo Gesualdo (c 1560-1613), and Claudio Monteverdi (1567-1643), are the most prominent names in this field.

Some of the later madrigalists devised pieces that presented a definite story, often in narrative form. These MADRIGAL COMEDIES were not intended to be acted on a stage—indeed, the music is so vivid they scarcely need the help of actors—but they are nevertheless forerunners of the seventeenth century opera. Alessandro Striggio (1535-1587), Orazio Vecchi (1550-1605), and Adriano Banchieri (1567-1634) are particularly associated with this type of madrigal.

Also of interest is the stream of light music that grew out of the fifteenth century frottola. Simple in style, and often so engagingly rhythmic they could be used for dancing, these pieces may be regarded as madrigals for the man-in-the-street. The most important of them is the BALLETTO, which was intended for singing and dancing, and makes use of the nonsense refrain 'Fa-la-la'. Giovanni Gastoldi (d.c 1622) is perhaps the most important composer of balletti.

The Italian madrigal was nowhere more admired than in England, where, at the end of the century, it took root and flourished for more than forty years. The English madrigal was no mere imitation of Italian models, however. It has many distinctive features of its own, and though arriving somewhat late on the scene it must be accounted an important contribution to European music.

The vogue for madrigals in England was enormous. Everybody with any claim to education and gentle breeding was expected to be able to join in singing them. An abundance of first-rate lyric poetry was an added stimulus to composition, and the English composers took advantage of it to produce a body of work that ranges over all the passions with equal skill and conviction. In terms of creative imagination the great English masters, Thomas Morley (1557-1603), John Wilbye (1574-1638), Thomas Weelkes (1575-1623), and Orlando Gibbons (1585-1625), are fully the equals of their Italian exemplars.

An important branch of English composition during this period is the AYRE—a song designed for performance by solo voice and lute, or for a group of self-supporting voices. The first published ayres were written by John Dowland (1536-1626), who remains perhaps the greatest master of the genre.

The madrigal did not take root in Germany, but her composers continued to write polyphonic songs in the tradition of the previous century. The POLYPHONIC LIED made considerable use of imitative techniques, and was often based on an existing popular tune. The leading composer in the first half of the century was Ludwig Senfl (c 1490-c 1556), and in the second half Hans Leo Hassler (1564-1612), who also wrote madrigals in the Italian manner.

During the Renaissance the demand for instrumental music increased rapidly. From this point in musical history onwards, composers show themselves more and more aware of instruments as instruments. They begin to search out and exploit their special characteristics. Instrumental music gradually establishes features that distinguish it radically from vocal music.

The instruments in general use at this time include *woodwind* (oboes and recorders of various sizes), *strings* (the members of the viol family), *brass* (trumpets and trombones), *plucked instruments* (lute and theorbo), *keyboard instruments* (the organ, large and small; harpsichord, virginals, and clavichord).

Instrumental ensembles came to be known as CONSORTS, and more often than not consisted of members of the same family—for example, a consort of viols, or a consort of recorders. Consorts of the same instruments were called 'whole' consorts, and of mixed families 'broken' consorts.

The music these instruments played can be divided into three basic categories: dance forms; instrumental forms adapted from or imitating vocal music; and forms that belong only to instruments.

Renaissance man enjoyed dancing, and during the sixteenth century many new types of dance were introduced. Very often pairs of dances were performed one after the other and were therefore thought of as belonging naturally to each other. Thus, at the beginning of the century we find the dignified PAVANE, a slow dance in duple time, linked with the lively GALLIARD, in triple time. By the middle of the century it was the turn of the PASSEMEZZO and SALTARELLO; and later still, the ALLEMANDE and COURANTE.

At dances these pieces were usually played by a consort of some kind. But they were also in demand as purely instrumental material, for lute, and the various keyboard instruments. In this secondary capacity they soon became very important. The practice of playing them in pairs (just as they had been danced in pairs) led to the idea of the DANCE SUITE—an extended group of contrasted dances. This, as we shall see, became the basis for many of the developments of the next century.

Equally fruitful was the tendency to elaborate the repeat of any section of the music by means of VARIATION. Nor should we forget that the essence of the dance—a strong, regular beat, and a bold melody that falls into neat, balancing sections—was to be the hall-mark of a style that dominated European music during the seventeenth, eighteenth and nineteenth centuries.

Much of the earliest printed instrumental music consists of direct transcriptions from vocal music: frottolas, chansons, motets, and so forth. The direct transcriptions were soon followed by purely instrumental pieces composed in the same style. A piece in the manner of a motet came to be known as a RICERCARE. The chanson gave rise to the CANZONA, which enjoys the same kind of contrasting sections and lively rhythms.

Ricercares and canzonas are to be found as keyboard music, lute music, and music for ensembles to play. The many fine examples by Andrea and Giovanni Gabrieli are particularly interesting because they explore the possibility of contrasting large and small groups of instruments, in much the same way as their vocal music made use of antiphonal choirs (see Chapter VII). In later years this technique was to form the basis of the concerto-grosso principle.

FANTASIAS, for keyboard, or ensemble groups, also made their appearance at this time. Like the ricercare and canzona, they stem from the imitative style of the motet and chanson. Instead of repeating or distinguishing between different sections of music, however, they flow on—one point of imitation growing out of another. Sometimes the entire composition depends on the cunning use of a single idea. It is this last variety of fantasia that was to develop, at the hands of Jan Pieterzoon Sweelinck (1562-1621),the last great Flemish composer, into the seventeenth-century fugue.

Independent instrumental forms of the period are rather less impressive. Mostly they are concerned with the search for a characteristic instrumental style, and are therefore filled with rapid scale passages, arpeggios, repeated notes, and the like. They seldom attempt to fill any particular formal shape. Such pieces are to be found under various titles: TOCCATA, PRELUDE, INTONAZIONE, for example.

The sixteenth century saw the first practical steps in music printing and publishing. Although he was not the first man to print music, Ottaviano dei Petrucci (1466-1539) is generally accepted as the first music-printer of technical and artistic genius. His first publication, the *Odhecaton,* dates from 1501, and during the next twenty years he issued no fewer than sixty-one volumes, containing music by all the great masters of the age.

Petrucci's publishing house in Venice was soon matched by similar ventures in Paris (Pierre Attaingnant, Pierre Haultin, and Robert Ballard), London (John Rastell, and John Gough), Antwerp (Christophe Plantin), and elsewhere.

The steady flow of printed music began to change the whole atmosphere of music-making. It was no longer the perogative of the very few who could afford the costly labour of a hand-copied manuscript. The influence a composer might have on his contemporaries was enormously increased as copies of his music sped to each corner of Europe. The world of music began to contract, and little by little the speed at which new developments could become the accepted property of all musicians began to increase. The printing presses had it in their power to revolutionize the art of music.

NOTES

NOTES

NOTES

PART THREE

Baroque
1600-1750

CHAPTER IX

THE NEW MONODIC STYLE

RENAISSANCE man, as we have seen, approached life with all the eagerness and wonder of a child set free to explore his surroundings for the first time. His successors, the men of the seventeenth century—the Baroque period, as it is sometimes called—took up a different point of view. They regarded the world not so much as a box of delights, as a stage whereon each must play his part. Their approach, and consequently their art, was self-aware, monumental, and frankly theatrical.

This delight in dramatic effect and theatrical magnificence can be seen in all the arts. In architecture, in the grandiose piazza of St Peter's, Rome, the splendour of Versailles, the calculated dignity of Sir Christopher Wren's St Paul's. In painting, in the breadth and drama of El Greco, Velasquez, Rubens, and, above all, Rembrandt. In literature, in the classic poise and rhetoric of Milton, Dryden, Racine, Corneille, and Molière.

Seventeenth century music also shares in this love of drama and grand design. Monumental and heroic in its proportions, vivid and realistic in its effects, it is a style that admirably expresses the spirit of the age.

The political background to these changes in European art is as complex and momentous as the art itself. England, torn by religious strife, and then by the battle between King and Parliament, quietly began to lay the foundations of an overseas empire and an international trade. For France, however, it was a period of active domination. She had emerged, after the religious upsets of the previous century, strong and integrated under the dazzle and brilliance of Louis XIV's absolute monarchy. Spain, by way of contrast, had soon lost all but the shadow of her sixteenth century glory. Germany continued as little more than an incoherent assembly of small states, racked by political and religious wars; and Italy remained divided into rival principalities.

Nevertheless, it was Italy that was the dominating influence in artistic matters. She derived her strength from the Catholic Church, whose authority, though challenged by Protestantism and the natural ambition of princes and monarchs to be seen as masters in their own countries, was still a power to be reckoned with. Indeed, much of the Baroque spirit in seventeenth century art is a reflection of Catholic vitality—the determination of the Church to do everything in her power to counteract the effects of the Reformation. It was only natural that she should marshal the tremendous emotional resources of the arts and turn them into an instrument for achieving these ends.

In music the Baroque attitude of mind is seen at its most characteristic in OPERA—the new and perhaps most important invention of the age. Beneath its expansive wings were ultimately assembled all those ingredients of drama, spectacle, and energetic realism that spell out the very essence of Baroque art. From it flowed nearly all the most important stylistic changes of the period.

The inventors of opera were members of one of the many Academies that had sprung up in Italy during the sixteenth century (see Chapter VIII). This group, the CAMERATA, met in Florence. They were much concerned with reviving the art of ancient Greek tragedy. One of their number, Vincenzo Galilei (the father of the great scientist), published his views in 1581, declaring that the elaborate polyphony of the Renaissance could not adequately express the meaning of words, and that it should therefore be replaced by a NUOVE MUSICHE—a new music.

This was to consist of a single melodic line that would imitate the natural rise and fall of speech, and would need to be supported only by a series of simple chords. Dramatic declamation of this kind, which follows the free rhythms of prose, is known as RECITATIVE; and the style of writing which confines the melodic interest to a single part, as MONODY.

Out of these conditions there arose the practice of writing figures beneath the bass line, to indicate the harmony that was to be placed between it and the melodic line floating above. This is known as FIGURED BASS, and the instruments concerned with its interpretation (usually a string bass instrument and a harpsichord, or organ) are called the BASSO CONTINUO.

The revolutionary aspect of this new style of composition can scarcely be over-stressed. From now on, music was not to be thought of as a texture woven from many different strands of melody, but as a tune, a bass line, and a filling of harmony in between. Chords could now be regarded as blocks of sound in their own right—each built up vertically from the bass line, and no longer merely the result of independent melodies passing one another.

Of course, the sound of music did not change over-night. Polyphony did not simply disappear. But the point of view from which music was regarded did change, and it was this, ultimately, that mattered.

The earliest example of a 'dramma per musica' (the term 'opera' was not yet in use) appears to have been *La Dafne*, written in 1597 by the poet Ottavio Rinuccini and set to music by Jacopo Peri. Unfortunately the music for this has been lost, and the work usually referred to as the first opera is *Euridice*, produced in 1600 by Rinuccini, Peri, and Guilio Caccini (also a composer) as part of the marriage celebrations of Maria de' Medici and Henry IV of France. In the same year a religious opera, *La rappresentazione di anima e di corpo*, was produced in Rome, with music by another member of the Camerata, Emilio de' Cavalieri.

The Peri-Caccini work consists mainly of long stretches of recitative, accompanied by a figured bass (interpreted, it seems, by a harpsichord, two lutes, and a viola da gamba). Very occasionally this recitative hardens into a simple formal pattern that suggests a definite 'song'.

Cavalieri's score, on the other hand, makes room for tuneful songs, brief choruses, dances, and instrumental interludes. It is therefore a much more interesting and colourful kind of work. And it was precisely this combination of ingredients which, together with recitative, were to be exploited by the first great operatic master: Claudio Monteverdi (1567-1643).

Unlike the more dogmatic of the Florentine monodists, Monteverdi was willing to press all the styles and techniques of his day into the service of opera. Fused into an integrated whole by his genius for expressing drama and emotion in terms of melody, harmony, and orchestral colour, the result could not fail to be impressive. His three surviving operas, *Orfeo* (Mantua, 1607), *Il Ritorno d'Ulisse*, and *L'Incoronazione di Poppea* (Venice, 1641 and 1642), rank as masterpieces. In them we can see, firmly established and made practical, the basic formula for all opera: the ARIA, an expressive melody organised into some definite shape; the ARIOSO, which is fairly melodic, but shares the formal freedom of recitative; the RECITATIVE itself, accompanied either by a continuo group or, when dealing with more emotional ideas, by an orchestra; instrumental interludes (SINFONIE); the early form of OVERTURE (the SINFONIA 'avanti l'opera'); ENSEMBLES (duets, trios, and so forth), and brief CHORUSES.

The idea of opera spread rapidly throughout Italy. The first public opera house, the Teatro San Cassiano, was established in Venice in 1637, and many more followed. Schools of opera composers soon became associated with the main cities in Italy. In Venice itself, for example, there were, besides Monteverdi, Francesco Cavalli (1602-1676), Marc Antonio Cesti (1623-1669), and Giovanni Legrenzi (1626-1690). The main centre of Italian opera in its later stages, however, was Naples, which grew to fame through the genius of Alessandro Scarlatti (1660-1725) and the practical resource of the many singing schools that flourished there.

The typical Neapolitan opera glorified the singer. In consequence, its structure revolved entirely around the aria and recitative. There were few choruses; and, apart from the occasional duet for the principal characters, few ensembles. Thus the pattern of each opera grew to be extremely formal and conventional. An operatic scene would consist of a recitative, which carried the drama forward a step, and an aria, which expressed the emotions that arose as a result. And so the plot unfolded, scene by scene, step by step, in a steady sequence of recitative and aria.

Furthermore, Baroque aesthetics held that each aria was to be governed by a single mood, or 'affection'. If an aria began by expressing despair, it must end by expressing despair—with the result that the drama stood still while the aria was being sung. In writing the words, all the operatic librettist could do to avoid monotony was to make sure that each aria dealt with a different mood from the one previously expressed.

Most arias were cast in the simple three-part form known as the DA CAPO ARIA, which consisted of a main section, a contrasting section, and a return of the main section with new vocal decorations. The singer was expected to add these vocal embellishments himself. They were of the utmost importance, for not only did they reveal the singer's skill, but they helped to rescue the rather obvious form from any danger of monotony, and generally served to heighten the emotional impact it could make.

Two further elements that developed in Neapolitan opera are also of importance: the so-called ITALIAN OVERTURE that preceded the opera; and the practice of introducing comic characters into serious opera (most operatic plots were based on classical mythology and were either tragic or heroic).

The overture was normally made up of three contrasting sections: the first being lively, and in canzona style, with strong rhythms; the second, slow and chordal in texture; and the third, fairly fast and in dance rhythm. This fast-slow-fast plan reflects the contrasting movements of the dance suite (see Chapter VIII). Eventually it became the starting point for the development of the classical symphony.

The comic characters, introduced at first simply for the sake of contrast, gradually became more and more important. By about 1700 they can be found linked in a story of their own, inserted as an INTERMEZZO between the acts of a serious work. By the 1730's these interludes had begun to appear as operas in their own right.

Unlike the OPERA SERIA, this new class of entertainment, the OPERA BUFFA, drew its material from everyday life. It used simple, folk-like tunes to enliven realistic, down-to-earth stories. Its enormous vitality proved to be a reforming influence that was to save serious opera from stifling in its own conventions.

Except in France, Italian opera conquered wherever it went. At the Viennese court, Johann Joseph Fux (1660-1730) cultivated Italian opera in a modified form—using more choruses and ensembles, and a generally more learned style. Vienna was also the headquarters of the poets Apostolo Zeno and Pietro Metastasio, whose libretti set the standard pattern for all Italian opera and were used over and over again by composers right up to the end of the eighteenth century.

In Germany, despite the misgivings of the more extreme Protestants, a school of Italian opera flourished for a time in Hamburg—coming to the climax of its achievements in the work of Reinhard Keiser (1674-1739) and Georg Friedrich Handel (1685-1750). While in Dresden, Johann Adolph Hasse (1699-1783) made equally brilliant contributions in the Italian manner. In their operatic work even the finest German masters were willing to pose as Italians—excelling, often, the very composers whose style they copied.

Italian opera also flourished in England, mostly at the hands of imported specialists, of whom the most influential was Handel. English composers themselves were rather slow to make use of the new ideas, and generally rejected whole-hearted recitative and lyricism. Their early experiments can be seen in the court MASQUE—an entertainment consisting of songs, dances, dialogue, and lavish scenic effects.

Indeed, England had almost achieved an operatic style of her own in the work of Matthew Locke (c 1630-1677), John Blow

(1649-1708), and Henry Purcell (c 1659-1695). Unfortunately popular demand was split between the taste for imported Italian opera on the one hand, and home-grown SEMI-OPERA (plays with music) on the other. Had Purcell lived longer the story might have been different. As it was, the only native style that was able to withstand the Italian invasion was the one that set up in direct opposition to it: the BALLAD OPERA. This, like the opera buffa, is opera of the people—stories from everyday life, with dialogue and simple tunes, many of which were borrowed from folk-song. A similar type of opera (the SINGSPIEL) arose, in direct imitation, in Germany towards the middle of the eighteenth century.

Only France stood out against the tide of Italian opera. French musical culture was centred on Paris, and was therefore largely dictated by the needs of Louis XIV's court. At first, BALLET DE COURT was the order of the day. This was dominated by dancing, in which members of the royal family often took part, and spectacular scenery. Dialogue, at first spoken but later sung in recitative, linked the various scenes. During the second half of the century this developed into the COMÉDIE-BALLET of Lully and Molière, which combined music and dancing with a humorous play.

The creation of French opera is almost entirely due to the fact that Lully's musical genius was fired by inordinate ambition and a keen sense of business. By 1684 he had so ingratiated himself with the king that no opera could be performed in France without his express permission. Thus, having blocked Italian competition, he proceeded to create an operatic style of his own.

Fortunately he was a man of genius, and his work proved worthy of French musical and literary traditions. The librettos he chose were of high literary quality and he respected them. His recitatives are models of correct declamation, and his arias much simpler in style than the florid 'singer's-aria' favoured by the Italians. Chorus, orchestra, and dance were all admitted as important ingredients; and despite the fact that each opera contrived to pour flattery over the king, the general level of dramatic common-sense and realism is much greater than was possible under the conventions of Italian opera.

Of particular importance is the typical Lullian overture—the FRENCH OVERTURE. This fell into two distinct sections: the first being slow and stately and characterised by the use of dotted rhythms; and the second, fast and fugal (imitative) in style. It

Monody: recitative from the opera *Orfeo* (1609) by Monteverdi

Expressive, conversational vocal lines, set against simple chords derived from a figured bass (this version is by Denis Stevens, published by Novello). The change of tonality in the seventh bar is a stroke of theatrical genius.

Messenger: Orpheus, miserable messenger of tidings yet more miserable and more tragic. Your lovely Euridice . . .
Orpheus: Alas, what do I hear?
Messenger: Your beloved wife is dead.
Orpheus: Woe is me.

The polyphony of J. S. Bach: *Fugue in E major* (No 9 from Book 2 of the '48')
Bach's smooth polyphony is controlled by strong harmonic progressions—the vertical and horizontal meet on equal terms.

The polyphony of J. S. Bach: chorus from the *St Matthew Passion*
Bach's harmonic counterpoint frequently rises to an expression of great emotional intensity—as in this setting of the words: *Truly, this was the Son of God.*

typifies the refined, aristocratic approach of French opera, as compared with the more immediate delights of Italy.

The classical grandeur of Lully's style was not wholly maintained by his successors, of whom Jean Philippe Rameau (1683-1761) is the most important. They preferred a more obviously 'pretty' kind of music, full of elegant, highly decorated melodies and, in Rameau's case particularly, an abundance of expressive orchestral effects. Their music reflects the intricate, highly emotional architecture of the Rococo period—itself a flowering of Baroque.

Closely allied to the opera, and an equally important expression of monodic ideals, was the chamber cantata: the CANTATA DA CAMERA.

The word 'cantata' simply meant that the music is sung—as opposed to the SONATA, which is played by instruments. The cantata, beginning as a dramatic monody in the period of Peri and Caccini, gradually developed, like opera itself, into a string of recitatives and arias—usually the personal monologue of one character. Needless to say, cantatas were not performed on the stage, but were chamber music pure and simple. In Germany a form of religious cantata, the CHURCH CANTATA, grew, as we shall see, to be of great importance.

CHAPTER X

CHURCH MUSIC IN THE SEVENTEENTH CENTURY

IN the face of competition from the new monodic style the vocal polyphony which had reached such remarkable heights in the work of Josquin, Palestrina, William Byrd, and their contemporaries, fell into rapid decline. When composers made use of it—and almost all of them did at one time or another—they did so out of respect for the past, and because the main centres of Catholic worship still regarded it as the true music of the church. Elsewhere, and particularly in Protestant countries, the more go-ahead clergy seized on the new dramatic style as an exciting and persuasive means of attracting the less enthusiastic members of their flock.

Much of the great religious music of the Baroque period

is not church music in the strict sense. There is now a distinct division between religious music (music with a religious theme) and liturgical music (music for a church service)—a division that was to grow with time.

Baroque church music retained some of the old features, but added new elements that were typical of monody. Soloists, independent instrumental material, figured bass accompaniments: all made their appearance. Latin gave way to the language of the country, and the universal style of the Renaissance became a variety of styles that reflect national origins.

In Italy the effects of colour and contrast to be found in the music of Andrea and Giovanni Gabrieli (see Chapter VIII) pointed the way. Whereas Palestrina and his contemporaries had exploited a smooth, seamless texture, woven from interlocking phrases, the Venetian masters had so disposed their forces as to make the most of contrasting sonorities. Sudden change was the very basis of their style. Inevitably it suggests the turbulence of human passion rather than the calm assurance of religious faith.

Monteverdi was the last great Italian master to write any considerable body of church music. His successors were operatic composers who wrote for the church when called upon, but seldom with much enthusiasm. Their efforts mostly relapse into an imitation of Palestrina—the revered 'stilo antico'. Monteverdi's work, on the other hand, reveals a remarkable attempt to wed Palestrinian orthodoxies to the emotional surge of the new music. In his collection of *Vesper Psalms and Motets* (1610), traditional plainsong is set, as a cantus firmus, against backgrounds of orchestral music, elaborate antiphonal dialogues for chorus, florid operatic melodies, and all the devices a highly developed sense of drama had led him to explore in his secular music.

By the middle of the seventeenth century the word 'motet' had come to mean almost any piece of music set to a Latin text, regardless of whether it followed traditional polyphony, or made use of recitative, da capo arias, orchestral interludes, and the whole paraphernalia of operatic technique. Within a hundred years the mass itself had succumbed to the style of the opera house—even though such interpretations played havoc with its function in the church liturgy.

In France, Louis XIV's impatience with the lengthy ceremonial of a complete mass led to the development of the MESSE BASSE SOLENELLE—low mass, with motets for voices and instruments as part of the otherwise plain service. Again, contrasting choirs, solo voices, and orchestral interludes make their appearance, underlining the enthusiasm with which Italian methods were adopted. The most important composers of church music in France, after Lully, were: Marc-Antoine Charpentier (1634-1704), Michel de la Lande (1657-1726), and François Couperin (1668-1733).

Since choral services were forbidden by the Puritans, English church music was unable to develop in any direction until after the restoration of the monarchy. During his exile in France, King Charles II had come to admire the new fashions in music. On returning, he let it be known that he would prefer to hear something like it in his own Chapel Royal. Therefore although the most important English composers of the day (John Blow and Henry Purcell) both composed FULL ANTHEMS in the old polyphonic style, they also began to explore the possibilities of the new music in their VERSE ANTHEMS.

In these, arias accompanied by continuo alternate with choral sections accompanied by strings. Orchestral interludes abound, and the introductory overture is a commonplace. And although the choral style retains much of the older polyphonic approach, the vivid drama of operatic techniques is very much in evidence.

In contrast to the somewhat uneasy position of liturgical music, the development of 'religious' music in England, Italy, and Germany proceeded swiftly and with confidence. The two forms it took, the ORATORIO and the CANTATA, reflect the true obsession of the age: drama in music.

Oratorio, which appeared in Italy at the same time as opera, seems to have originated with the Catholic Church's anxiety to do what the new Protestant Church had done: bring the facts of religion to the notice of ordinary men and women in some easily understood and attractive form. It took its name from the 'Oratorio', a public meeting place in Rome where the followers of St Philip Neri (1515-1595) gathered to pray, hear sermons, and sing hymns. Some of the hymns they sang were in dialogue form, and the earliest oratorios were simply an extension of the same idea. Within a very short time there had grown up a religious drama, with words sung in arioso style by the characters, a narrator to hold the story together, and a chorus to comment on the ideas that were being expressed.

Although oratorio took over some of the dramatic tricks of opera it remained a non-stage form, and always laid great stress on the use of a chorus. Its first great master was Giacomo Carissimi (1605-1674).

Oratorio made its appearance in Germany in the work of

Heinrich Schütz (1585-1672). But undoubtedly the most famous and important developments took place in England under Handel, whose long series of oratorios, begun only after he had failed to established his Italian operas, raised the form to its greatest heights.

Handel's oratorios combine the melodic grace of Italian opera with the intellectual strength of German polyphony and the robust vigour of English choral writing. The result proved so irresistible to the English that it remained a dominating, and indeed a stifling influence for more than a hundred years.

Unlike their Italian contemporaries, who turned away from the original source and mainstay of their religious music (the plainchant), German composers were profoundly influenced by the 'official' music of their new Protestant religion. The importance of the Lutheran chorale in shaping the various forms of religious music in Germany can scarcely be exaggerated. It left its mark on vocal and instrumental music alike, and there were few composers who did not respond to its sturdy, independent nature.

The ways in which a chorale might be treated as a basis for vocal composition can be seen in the work of Michael Praetorius (1571-1621). In his collection of chorale compositions, the nine volumes of *Musae Sioniae* (1601), he describes three methods of approach. They are: the 'chorale-motet', in which each phrase of the chorale is used as a point of imitation, thus producing the old-style polyphonic texture; the 'madrigal-style', in which the chorale is broken into small motives that are then used to create a dialogue between different groups of voices; and the 'cantus-firmus chorale', in which the chorale itself appears in long notes, with the other parts weaving an independent texture around it. Later, Praetorius adapted the ideas of Gabrieli and set the chorale for alternating solo and choral groups, sometimes adding instrumental interludes.

Similar experiments are to be seen in the work of Johann Hermann Schein (1586-1630), Samuel Scheidt (1578-1654), and, most notably, Heinrich Schütz (1585-1672). The desire to bring out the dramatic truth of the chorale words led to experiments in monody and ensemble, and these, combined with the use of contrasting choral groups and instrumental interludes, led to the gradual evolution of a distinctly German kind of cantata.

The CHORALE CANTATA, developing in the work of Heinrich Schütz, Franz Tunder (1614-1667), Dietrich Buxtehude (1637-1707), Georg Böhm (1661-1733), and Johann Pachelbel (1653-1706), reached great heights in the music of Johann Sebastian

Bach (1685-1750). The variety of style to be found in these composers, and in Bach in particular, is enormous. Overtures and instrumental interludes, massive choral movements in concerto style (see Chapter XI), dances and fugues, recitative, arias, duets and trios, elaborate contrapuntal devices—all found their way into the church cantata, making it one of the richest and most fruitful expressions of the age, the country, and the faith.

Equally important is the development of German settings of the PASSION—the Crucifixion story, as recorded in the different gospels. Passions had been presented in dramatic form as early as the twelfth century, and gradually they had developed into a recital of the gospel narrative (sung to a special chant), with a chorus adding comments from time to time. The addition of an orchestral and organ accompaniment brought the passion into line with the early oratorio. From there it was but a simple step to incorporating all the dramatic devices of opera—recitative, aria, and so forth. These, of course, served to emphasize all the lurid and sentimental aspects of the story. But in an age which revelled in operatic extravagance such liberties were much appreciated. The OPERA-PASSIONS engaged the attentions of German composers throughout the eighteenth century.

Bach's settings of the passion story present a very different picture. Though they make full use of the dramatic style of the time, they do so with restraint and true reverence. Chorales are used, both in simple four-part harmonisation, and in all the variety of elaborate treatment to be found in the cantatas. The use of the chorus is particularly striking—being organised, often, into large-scale movements of great complexity.

Somewhat apart from the rest of his religious music are Bach's settings of Latin texts: the *Magnificat* (1723), and the *B minor Mass* (1733). Both make use of plainchant cantus firmus, and both ignore the chorale. Though a devout Protestant, Bach evidently felt that the significance of the old Catholic texts went beyond the quibbles of religious sectarianism. At all events, both works are masterpieces of the very highest order.

CHAPTER XI
THE RISE OF INSTRUMENTAL MUSIC

FROM the middle of the seventeenth century, and for the first time in musical history, instrumental music began to assume as much importance as music written for voices. In consequence, a new musical style which exploited the special characteristics of the instruments themselves gradually came into existence. And because it was aimed at an audience, whose attention had not only to be attracted but held, this new kind of music had many distinctive features.

In the first place, it made use of musical ideas that were concise and easily remembered—short, pregnant motives that made their point with all the force of a decisive gesture. Secondly, it called upon new methods of holding a work together. For the most part, these are concerned with what may conveniently be called the 'architectural' shape of the music. That is to say: the effect brought about when recognisable sections of a musical structure are made to balance one another by means of deliberate contrast, repetition, and variation. These effects, though by no means absent in the music of earlier periods, were now made workable by changes in the vocabulary of music itself.

The most important of these was the change from modal music to KEY TONALITY.

During the previous hundred years or so, the distinction between the old church modes had gradually been eroded. Musicians had changed the patterns of these scales by introducing foreign notes, which they called MUSICA FICTA (they are the equivalent of our 'accidentals'). By the middle of the seventeenth century the alterations to the modes had become so general that they had in fact merged into two basic scale patterns: the Major and Minor DIATONIC SCALES. It was now possible to think in terms of identical scales, whatever the note chosen as a starting point might be.

But starting on different notes meant that each scale now identified a new area of sound. Each new series of notes therefore came to be thought of as a KEY. And, by simple adjustments, it was possible to move from one key area to another, in a kind of tonal journey. This process is called MODULATION.

Furthermore, the notes within each identical scale were all felt to have a special relationship with one another. Some were more important and therefore acted as focal points around which the others revolved. Of these fixed points of reference, the two most important were the first and fifth notes of the scale, known, respectively, as the TONIC and DOMINANT.

This new way of looking at the materials of music provided the basic principles upon which the new formal structures were built. The shape of a piece of music could now be reinforced by the way in which movement was made from key to key. Each section of the work could be identified with a particular key, and further made memorable by having its own musical ideas. Corresponding sections could make use of the same keys and the same ideas, thus throwing into relief those other sections intended as a contrast.

Along with these developments in the basic materials of music there came also radical changes in the kinds of musical texture they were required to serve. From now on, complex polyphony was at a discount. What mattered was a shapely tune, a firm bass line, and a filling of appropriate chords in between. We call this kind of music HOMOPHONIC (the parts all sounding together, as distinct from the independent strands of polyphony).

The seventeenth century saw a considerable increase in the demand for keyboard music. This is not, of course, surprising, for the keyboard is precisely the medium through which a homophonic style can be explored most easily.

For the harpsichord there was the DANCE SUITE: a group of stylised dances in contrasting rhythms and speeds, with the Allemande, Courante, Sarabande, and Gigue as almost invariable elements. Optional dances, mostly borrowed from French ballet, included the Gavotte, Bourée, Minuet, Rigaudon, and Passpied.

Most dance movements made use of the conventional two-part structure known as BINARY FORM. This consists of two balancing sections, the first moving into a related key (usually the dominant) and the second making the expected return journey. A few dances explored TERNARY FORM: a three-part structure, in which two similar (even identical) sections in the same key are separated by a contrasting middle section, in a different key.

The important composers of keyboard suites include: Froberger and Bach in Germany; Purcell and Handel in England; Couperin and Rameau in France. Couperin's harpsichord suites are particularly fine. They make a feature of elaborate and delicate ornamentation, and are often descriptive and supplied with fanciful titles.

To avoid monotony, the composers of harpsichord music seldom allowed the immediate repetition of a musical passage to follow the original, note for note. Instead, they added ornaments and decorations, and thus made a VARIATION upon it. In France such variations were called DOUBLES.

This device soon became a form in its own right: the THEME AND VARIATIONS, in which a simple tune (either borrowed, or the composer's own) was repeated several times in differently varied ways. Usually the variations were made to become progressively more elaborate, until a final climax resolved itself in a plain statement of the original tune.

A similar procedure can be found in the various GROUND BASS structures (the PASSACAGLIA, and CHACONNE, for example), where a simple melodic formula is repeated against a background of changing material.

During this period the word SONATA (meaning an instrumental piece, as opposed to the cantata, which was sung) began to be used to describe certain short keyboard works. The most important examples can be seen in the series that Domenico Scarlatti (1685-1757) wrote. They are one-movement pieces, mostly in binary form, and are particularly interesting for the way in which they exploit all manner of characteristic keyboard effects.

Movements in free styles and forms, known variously as PRELUDES, TOCCATAS, FANTASIAS, etc, were often used in the late seventeenth century as introductions to the strict formalities of a FUGUE—Bach's *48 Preludes and Fugues,* for example.

Arising out of the imitative style of the ricercare and canzona (see Chapter VIII), the fugue developed, in the hands of such composers as Frescobaldi, Froberger, Buxtehude, Böhm, and Bach, into a complex structure in which a number of parts (or voices) combine in stating and restating a single musical idea, in contrapuntal fashion. The resulting texture is very like that of the madrigal—except, of course, that only one 'point of imitation' is employed.

Strictly in terms of its own idiom, the organ shared certain of the harpsichord forms already mentioned. Preludes, fantasias, toccatas and fugues all made an appearance in Baroque organ music—often to added advantage, because of the organ's ability to sustain notes and build up great climaxes of massed sound.

In Germany considerable use was made of the chorale as a basis for organ music. Under the general description CHORALE PRELUDE, several types of treatment can be distinguished: making use, for example, of fugue, variation, free fantasia, and cantus firmus techniques. In each case, however, it was the chorale that supplied the material for the composition.

It is entirely in keeping with the expressive, self-dramatizing spirit of Baroque art that the bright, virtuoso tone of the VIOLIN family began to take precedence over the more restrained, intimate viols. Raised now from its original status as a dancing-master's instrument, the violin, thanks to the genius of Italian makers like Nicolo Amati and Antonio Stradivari, entered polite society, and in so doing brought into existence its own kind of music.

Although at this period the distinction is not always clearly maintained, instrumental music came to be divided into two classes: CHAMBER music (implying a small group of instruments, one to each part), and ORCHESTRAL music (implying a larger group, with the possibility of several instruments to a part).

Chamber music is to be found under two main headings. First, the SOLO SONATA, which consists of a solo instrument (usually a violin) supported by a figured bass accompaniment, played by the usual combination of harpsichord (or organ) and string bass. Second, the TRIO SONATA, employing two solo instruments, with continuo support. Both were made up of a number of contrasting movements, and are thus clearly indebted to the dance suite.

A solo or trio sonata that consisted entirely of movements in dance patterns was called a CHAMBER SONATA (Sonata da camera). One that incorporated more dignified, abstract movements was referred to as a CHURCH SONATA (Sonata da chiesa). In practice the distinction was not always strictly maintained, though most church sonatas begin with a solemn *adagio*, followed by an *allegro* in fugal style. The fact that the church sonata was often played during a service did not prevent it from making use of dance rhythms.

The solo and trio sonata developed mainly in Italy and Germany. In Italy the most outstanding names are those of Arcangelo Corelli (1653-1713), and Antonio Vivaldi (1680-1743). In Germany: Georg Philipp Telemann (1681-1767), and J. S. Bach. French chamber music is represented by Jean Marie Leclair (1697-1765), and English by Henry Purcell.

Although the difference between chamber and orchestral music could at times be conveniently vague and as much a matter of what instruments happened to be available as anything, a distinct orchestral style began to emerge in the seventeenth century.

The Baroque orchestra, consisting mainly of strings, played a considerable part in accompanying the larger vocal forms—opera, cantata, oratorio, etc. There, as we have seen, it developed forms of its own: in particular the Italian and French overtures. Movements built along these lines began also to appear as introductions to orchestral dance suites.

The most important orchestral form of the period, however, was the CONCERTO GROSSO.

Arranged, like a dance suite, as a series of contrasting movements, the concerto grosso owed its characteristic style to its instrumentation. This consisted of a main orchestra (the TUTTI, or RIPIENO), and a group of soloists (the CONCERTINO). Thus it was possible to exploit the idea of dynamic contrast—the slender sounds of the soloists alternating with passages for orchestra. The link between this principle and the antiphonal choirs of Renaissance music (see Chapter VII) is obvious.

Not every concerto grosso movement took advantage of the 'concerto principle', but those that did acquired a very particular formal shape. Beginning almost invariably with a bold orchestral tutti that stated the main musical idea in the clearest terms, the movement evolved through a series of repetitions of the opening material in different keys, separated by sections in which the concertino group took over. Sometimes the concertino group explored musical ideas of its own, sometimes it remained faithful to the ideas given out in the opening orchestral tutti.

This method of giving architectural shape to a movement by means of a returning theme is known as the RITORNELLO PRINCIPLE. In Baroque music it can be seen not only in the concerto grosso, but in the da capo aria, and the orchestral accompaniments to oratorio choruses.

The concerto grosso was developed mainly in Italy and Germany, by such composers as Corelli, Torelli, Geminiani, Vivaldi, Telemann, Bach, and Handel. Corelli probably did more to establish it in the first place than any other composer.

At the beginning of the eighteenth century, certain composers, who were themselves virtuoso players of instruments, began to explore the possibility of reducing the concertino group to a single instrument (often a violin). Inevitably the contrast between soloists and tutti could not be maintained with the original consistency or effect. The soloist tended, therefore, to play more continuously and in a rather more obviously virtuoso manner, thus bringing the form within hailing distance of practices that belong to the Classical period.

NOTES

NOTES

NOTES

NOTES

PART FOUR

Classical
1750-1827

CHAPTER XII

THE EIGHTEENTH CENTURY AND THE SONATA

THE second half of the eighteenth century is generally considered a period in which common sense and rational thought triumphed over ignorance and superstition. The facts, however, are not quite so simple, or so comforting. It is no accident that this serene century came to an end under the shadow of the French guillotine. Reason and restraint, the twin gods of the age, walked hand in hand with folly and excess.

Something of the same contradiction can be seen in the arts of the period. The mid-eighteenth century passion for classical studies encouraged a style of domestic architecture reflecting the clean, harmonious lines of ancient Greece—the homely dignity of John Wood's Bath, for example. But logic and common sense could as easily turn, by way of reaction, to the Gothick fantasies of Walpole's *Strawberry Hill,* or Beckford's *Fonthill.* In literature, the wild imagination of William Blake followed hard upon the studied, classical prose of Edward Gibbon and Dr Samuel Johnson. And in music, the moderation, balance, and proportion of Gluck, Haydn, and Mozart was swallowed up in the turbulent, revolutionary passions of Beethoven.

The description 'classical' for the art and outlook of the period is, therefore, true only up to a point. Emotional restraint, clarity of form, an agreed system of working-conventions, are all to be found. But we must not be surprised to see them overthrown, even by their firmest champions.

The music of the Classical period is dominated by a principle of composition that had first appeared during the early part of the century (see Chapter XI). This principle, or method of composition, sought to give music an almost tangible architectural shape, wherein corresponding sections, separated by appropriate contrasts, could be felt to balance each other, while pursuing at the same time a forward drive through a chain of logically connected keys. It found its main outlet in the creation of SONATA FORM.

In establishing this new approach to music, composers, as we have seen, largely abandoned old methods of composition. The free lines of polyphony gave way to homophonic textures: firm melodies built upon equally firm bass lines, with a solid filling of harmony in between. The melodies themselves gave up their long flowing lines to become simple, folk-like, and compact: shaped by clear, balancing phrases, and regular, dance-like rhythms. Counterpoint, though used, was of secondary importance, and its most characteristic forms fell into almost complete neglect.

The important developments in the new style took place in the field of instrumental music. The SYMPHONY and the SOLO CONCERTO were the main forms explored by the rapidly growing orchestra; while chamber music found its chief glory in the STRING QUARTET. Gradual improvements in the pianoforte (invented earlier in the century) led to a new preoccupation: the PIANO SONATA. The developments in church music are less impressive, but opera continued to challenge men of genius.

That the centre for these changes should have been Austria and the south German principalities is not surprising. Situated in the middle of Europe, these areas were open to influences from the south and from the north. The cheerful simplicity of Italian opera buffa made itself felt with as much force as the intellectual rigours of German counterpoint. Neither too sunny, nor too severe, the middle European temperament was exactly suited to create an amalgam of both extremes. The result—the sonata—swept the musical world and remained a dominating force for nearly one hundred and fifty years.

Sonata form, with certain modifications, is the basis for nearly all instrumental music from this period onwards. Moulded by the experiments of many composers it was eventually established as a group of three or four movements, built on well-defined lines.

The first movement is almost invariably an *allegro*. Its formal pattern is known either as SONATA (FIRST MOVEMENT) FORM, or SONATA-ALLEGRO FORM, and consists of three principal sections: the EXPOSITION, the DEVELOPMENT, and the RECAPITULATION. Sometimes a slow introduction is used as a preface to the main body of the movement.

In the exposition the composer establishes the musical material of the movement. A FIRST SUBJECT (or group of ideas) is presented

Eighteenth-century elegance: Mozart *Sonata in D major* (K 576)
A delicate, ornamental style—though shot through with Mozart's steely strength of purpose. Basically homophonic, with modest touches of polyphonic imitation.

Nineteenth-century passion: Beethoven *Sonata in F minor* (Appassionata)
Compare this extract with the Mozart example. Beethoven's violence and emotional intensity is immediately obvious—the keyboard is treated almost as a miniature orchestra.

in the key of the sonata (the tonic key). A BRIDGE PASSAGE then modulates to a new key (that of the dominant if the sonata is in a major key, and the relative-major in the case of minor keys). A SECOND SUBJECT (or group of ideas) is then presented in the new key.

The principle involved in a sonata exposition is that of contrast: contrast of thematic material, and contrast of key. First and second subject groups necessarily belong to each other, in that they are events in a logical progress of musical thought. But they must also express a recognisable difference in character. In the same way, the keys are closely related, while at the same time being fundamentally different. The principle of contrast is in itself an expression of dramatic conflict, and it is this that lies at the root of sonata thinking.

The classical exposition normally ends with double bars and a repeat sign. After the repetition the composer begins to explore the possibilities latent in the thematic ideas of the exposition. This, the development section, follows no set pattern, but invariably modulates through several keys and establishes, in its treatment of the themes, the idea of growth through logical argument.

The recapitulation consists of a re-statement of the exposition's thematic material entirely in the tonic key. The bridge passage, of course, is altered to accomodate this change of tonal direction.

The second movement is, by way of contrast, lyrical and song-like. It is usually in a slow tempo, and very often extremely simple in structure—a complex structure would only hinder the lyricism. Ternary, rondo, and variation patterns are very common, though sometimes a simplified sonata-allegro form is used.

The third movement borrows from the dance suite. It is a straight-forward minuet and trio, moderately fast and in three-four time. The pattern: minuet—trio—minuet, gives an overall ternary shape, in which each section may itself fall into a binary or ternary form.

The last movement returns again to the lively tempo and tonic key of the opening movement. Light-hearted rondo forms were popular, and certainly provide the right kind of cheerful conclusion. Sonata-allegro patterns, however, are also common.

The four movement plan is to be found in most classical symphonies and quartets, and in some keyboard sonatas. The solo concerto, however, traditionally omits the minuet and trio—possibly because its dance qualities told against the effective exchange between solo instrument and orchestra.

It is not hard to appreciate the all-embracing nature of sonata form, or the challenge it presented to every aspect of a composer's technique. The lyricism of the slow movement, the lively pulse of the dance, the cheerful bustle of the finale, and the logical argument demanded by the first movement were tests that not every composer could rise to with equal skill.

Above all, it was a musical form that actively explored the idea of organic growth. Its material *becomes* something new, in the same way that a drama unfolds. And this was a revolutionary concept in music.

CHAPTER XIII
THE SYMPHONY AND THE CONCERTO

MANY attractive theories have been advanced to account for the origins and growth of the classical symphony. But they remain, stubbornly, theories, open to contradiction. If it were a matter merely of observing the contribution made by the three great men of genius who brought it to perfection—Haydn, Mozart, and Beethoven—then all would be plain sailing. But they also learned their art, and learned it from the example of their many contemporaries. Thus it can only be that dozens of lesser men helped to create the symphony, to which these three brought the final authority of genius.

In the eighteenth century, symphonic form was in the air. All the ingredients were to hand: a homophonic style, the possibility of contrast and tension between keys, a type of melody that was clear-cut and incisive, a rapidly developing orchestra, a demand for music that would entertain the senses, satisfy the intellect, and embody the emotions of the new, middle-class audience. The symphony came into existence not because of any decision on the part of individual composers, but because it answered the needs and inclinations of an age.

The word 'symphony' is derived from the Italian 'sinfonia', which had earlier been used to describe almost any kind of instrumental music. Its particular application to the operatic overture (see Chapter IX) would seem to be the starting point for any inquiry into the origins of the symphony.

Italian and French overtures consisted, as we have seen, of two or three contrasted movements. Such works might easily be played as independent orchestral pieces away from their parent operas. From there it was but a short step to the composition of similar works, intended only for the concert hall. This, then, was the probable line of development: the need for concert music arose and was satisfied from the nearest source to hand, and then further supplied by imitation. The term 'sinfonia' stayed with the music of the concert hall, and the opera adopted 'overture' (literally 'opening') as the proper description for its introductory music. In the middle of the eighteenth century it was perfectly possible for a composer to use the same work both as an 'overture' and as a 'sinfonia'. The forms were identical.

Gradually, however, the contrasting movements of the sinfonia began to assert typical formal patterns. Of these the most important was the sonata-allegro plan (see Chapter XII). Probably this was evolved from the binary structures typical of the dance suite, and the one-movement sonatas of Domenico Scarlatti.

Binary form, as we have seen, embraces two balancing sections of music: the first moving to the dominant (or relative minor) key, and the second making the return journey to the tonic. In some examples the closing bars of the first section are repeated at the end of the second section, thus giving a kind of musical rhyme. It needs only a slight extension of this practice (a clearer effect of definition to the rhyming phrase) to suggest the main principle of mature sonata-allegro form: a theme associated with the tonic key, in contrast with a different theme associated with the dominant, or relative minor.

Moreover, not all binary structures made the return to the tonic a precise mirror of the opening section. Some allowed a considerable digression before the return was made, often passing through different keys. In this we may recognise a 'development section' in embryo.

Among the dozens of composers who helped to create the early symphony, mention must be made of: Giovanni Battista Sammartini (1698-1775), who taught Gluck, J. C. Bach, and Mozart; the composers associated with the court orchestra at Mannheim: Johann Stamitz (1717-1757) and his two sons Karl and Anton, Ignaz Holzbauer (1711-1783), and Christian Cannabich (1731-1798); the Viennese, Georg Monn (1717-1750), Georg Wagenseil (1715-1777), and Karl Ditters von Dittersdorf (1739-1799); Bach's sons, Carl Philipp Emanuel Bach (1714-1788), and Johann Christian Bach (1735-1782); and the Frenchman, François Gossec (1734-1829).

Once the symphonic idea had gained currency it spread like wildfire, and there were few countries that could not boast home-grown examples. London, for example, which enjoyed the services of such foreigners as J. C. Bach and Karl Friedrich Abel (1723-1787), could call upon the talents of Thomas Augustine Arne (1710-1778) and William Boyce (1710-1779). Even remote Stockholm produced a respectable symphonist in Johan Helmich Roman (1694-1758).

Of particular importance to the symphony's early development was the work accomplished by the Mannheimers. There, at the court of Duke Carl Theodor, a remarkable orchestra was built up. In 1756 it consisted of 10 first violins, 10 seconds, 4 violas, 4 cellos, 2 basses, 4 flutes, 2 oboes, 2 bassoons, and 4 horns—together with a corps of 12 trumpets and 2 drums for special occasions. It was famous throughout Europe, not only for its size, but also for the precision of its playing. The musical historian Dr Charles Burney declared: 'there are more solo players, and good composers in this, than perhaps in any other orchestra in Europe; it is an army of generals. . . .'

Most orchestras of the period consisted of strings, oboes, and horns. Flutes, bassoons, trumpets, and, towards the end of the century, clarinets, were added whenever circumstances allowed. To begin with, the harpsichord continuo was used as an essential binding-agent. It was the centre from which the performance could be controlled—there were no conductors as such, the direction came from the leader of the violins, and the continuo player. Only gradually and towards the end of the century did the woodwind section become self-supporting; and it was not until the beginning of the nineteenth century that the brass section was able to stand on its own feet.

The example of the Mannheim orchestra helped to set a standard throughout Europe. It excelled in producing expressive and dramatic orchestral effects: *crescendos, diminuendos,* contrasts between *piano* and *forte,* and all manner of theatrical tricks calculated to excite the attentions of a new and growing public. The Mannheim composers aimed at broad effects: bold themes, built on the notes of the common chord and articulated by spirited rhythms; simple background accompaniments that kept the music alive, but did not distract the mind with useless detail. It was a new kind of music, and the appeal was frankly popular.

The early symphonies, following the operatic overture, mostly favoured a three-movement plan. By the middle of the eighteenth century a fourth movement had become common—a minuet and trio, placed immediately after the slow movement, and borrowed, of course, from the dance suite.

It must now be clear that Franz Joseph Haydn (1732-1809) and Wolfgang Amadeus Mozart (1756-1791) did not invent the symphony. They did, however, bring it to a state of perfection.

Both learned from their contemporaries and from each other. Both made individual contributions. Haydn in terms of structural ingenuity and inventiveness, and Mozart in terms of sheer elegance and expressive beauty. Between them they produced a stream of symphonies which surpass anything that had been written by even the most gifted of their contemporaries.

In their work the dramatic possibilities inherent in symphonic methods are, for the first time, clearly realised. The contrast between themes with different characters, and between opposing key areas becomes the means of dramatic conflict and musical argument. The mature symphonies of Haydn and Mozart are more than mere vehicles for entertainment. They are intellectual and emotional experiences, forceful expressions of personality, the quintessence of their creators' originality.

Neither men were content with the simple homophonic methods of their predecessors. Both turned to the techniques of polyphony, and found in its devices of imitation and fugue a means of articulating and giving significance to the texture of their music. Although their symphonic style retained the peculiar benefits of homophony (bold tunes, and a strong procession of harmonies), it was also shot through with the animating force of polyphonic exchange. They spread the musical interest throughout the texture, thus achieving the kind of complexity which alone can carry the burden of deep thought and emotion. It is upon the foundations they laid that Beethoven was able to build.

A similar pattern of development took place in the field of the concerto. We have already noted (see Chapter XI) the tendency on the part of later Baroque composers to reduce the concertino element in the concerto grosso to a single instrument. Such works frequently consisted of three movements, and, being similarly based on the idea of an exchange of material between a solo instrument and an orchestra, they are obvious precursors of the classical solo concerto.

The main distinguishing feature of the classical concerto is its adoption of a modified sonata-allegro structure for the first movement. Again, many hands contributed towards this solution —in particular those of C. P. E. Bach and J. C. Bach. But it was Mozart who brought the form to its first state of perfection.

As always in matters of musical form, it is impossible to pin down one definitive shape that will cover every experiment that genius may throw up. In general terms, however, the first movement of the typical Mozart piano concerto combines the legacy of a recurring orchestral ritornello (inherited from the concerto grosso) with the basic outline and key-plan of the new sonata-allegro structure.

The second movement is usually slow in tempo, and given over to gentle lyricism—simple ternary forms, sets of variations, and so forth are appropriate. The third movement is again fast, and almost always cheerful—the rondo pattern, more often than not.

The real formal problems, then, occur in the first movement. The classical solution was to present a sonata-allegro with a double exposition: one for the orchestra alone, with both first and second subjects in the tonic key; and one for the soloist and orchestra together, with the subjects in the usual related keys. New material was frequently introduced during the course of the second exposition, for the sake of variety.

The subsequent development and recapitulation sections followed the normal sonata-allegro plan, with soloist and orchestra sharing the work on equal terms. Towards the end of the recapitulation the soloist was allowed to break away for a moment, to indulge in an unaccompanied, free CADENZA—often improvised on the spot.

It is important to note that the various stages in unfolding the concerto's sonata-allegro structure are all marked off by the emphatic return of an orchestral tutti. The exposition opens and closes with an orchestral statement; the development is interspersed with brief tutti returns; the recapitulation opens with an orchestral tutti; and a tutti rounds off the entire movement. The similarity between this feature and the general style of the concerto grosso movement is obvious.

During the second half of the eighteenth century there was an enormous increase in the amount of music intended for day-to-day entertainment. Besides music for dancing, there was music to accompany meals, music to be listened to beneath the trees of the Pleasure Gardens—music, in short, to fill every social need. It is to be found under a variety of names: SERENADE, NACHTMUSIK, CASSATION, DIVERTIMENTO, and so on. Though the movements might borrow from symphonic forms (treating them in an appropriately more superficial way), simple dance patterns make up the generality. Such works are the equivalent of the Baroque dance suite.

By the same token, music written for small groups of solo instruments was also in great demand—music, that is, for the intelligent listener. The chief media for chamber music, replacing the Baroque string fantasia, trio sonata, and solo sonata, were the STRING QUARTET, the VIOLIN SONATA, and the PIANO SONATA. Each made use of the conventional sonata plan—the string quartet developing as a four-movement work, and the violin and piano sonatas as three-movement works.

The string quartet is by far the most important of the three. It developed alongside the symphony, sharing its general structure, but necessarily exploring a more intimate kind of music. The problem of thinking in terms of four equal voices (two violins, a viola, and a cello) was a challenge that only the greatest masters could rise to. Shoddy thinkers soon revealed the poverty of their ideas in such exposed conditions. Inevitably, then, the greatest contributions came from Haydn, Mozart, and Beethoven.

Similar in structure and method are certain other combinations: notably, the mixed quartet (three strings and one other instrument—a piano perhaps, or a flute); the string trio (violin, viola, and cello); the mixed trio (violin, cello, and piano); the string quintet (two violins, two violas, and cello); and the mixed quintet. Each combination had its attractions and posed its own problems, but for one reason or another failed to suggest itself to most composers as the perfect medium for intimate, searching musical thought. That honour fell to the string quartet.

CHAPTER XIV
OPERA IN THE EIGHTEENTH CENTURY

WHATEVER convention may have demanded in the way of church music, the religious impulse of the eighteenth century does not seem to have been strong enough to have sparked off more than a routine response from even the greatest composers. Such moments of truth as did occur came, almost invariably, in answer to some direct challenge from this world, rather than from mystical absorption in the affairs of the next.

The church music of the Classical period was basically dramatic in conception. Much of it seems more suited for performance on the concert platform than for use as part of the church liturgy. Despite Papal indignation, the mass was often treated to full-scale concert settings for chorus, soloists, and orchestra—complete with every operatic device from showy aria to 'realistic' orchestral commentary. This was what the eighteenth century patron wanted of his composers, and, since he controlled the conditions of performance and paid the bill, he was at liberty to call the tune.

Yet the fault lay not only with the patron. Even genuinely reverent composers (such as Haydn) were betrayed into attempting effects of musical unity that ran counter to the religious sense of the words they wished to set. There is nothing, for example, in the words of any part of the mass that suggests the shape of a sonata-allegro movement. But sonata-allegro patterns regularly appear in eighteenth century masses. It is as if the composer's genuine passion was for music and purely musical problems, with no room left for spiritual subtleties—an attitude wholly in keeping with an 'age of reason'.

At moments, however, the façade of spiritual unconcern crumbles and raw emotion shows through. Significantly this happens, more often than not, when the religious message touches upon some urgent temporal problem. Haydn's *Mass in time of War*, written under the shadow of Napoleon's invading armies, is an urgent and moving cry for deliverance. The tradition is continued in Beethoven's *Missa Solemnis*.

In vocal music the real genius of the age went into opera. Two men dominated the scene: Christoph Willibald Gluck (1714-1787), and Wolfgang Amadeus Mozart.

Although the heroic conventions of opera seria still persisted in the work of many eighteenth century composers, the general tendency of the period was towards a less formal, more realistic approach, both in terms of music and drama. In an age that prized commonsense, and was moving towards an acceptance of democracy, this is hardly surprising. The stiff formalities of Baroque opera might accord very well with the rigid etiquette of Bourbon and Hapsburg court life, but they could hardly be expected to appeal to the rising middle-class. What did appeal, of course, were the various forms of comic opera (see Chapter IX).

But it would be wrong to assume that opera seria vanished from the scene. It persisted and was admired, along with the singers that were its chief glory. Comic opera had a long way to go before it could be universally accepted as a respectable form of entertainment.

Most composers were at home with both kinds of opera, and switched from one style to the other as the occasion demanded. Such men include: Niccolo Jommelli (1714-1744), Tommaso Traetta (1727-1779), Antonio Sacchini (1730-1786), Nicolo Piccinni (1728-1800), Domenico Cimarosa (1749-1801), and Giovanni Paisiello (1740-1816), among the Italians; and François Philidor (1726-1795), Pierre Monsigny (1728-1817), and André Grétry (1742-1813), among the French.

The need for operatic reform, implicit in the spontaneous flowering of comic opera, found its more calculated expression in the work of Gluck and Mozart. They approached the problem in quite different ways. Gluck's reforms were the result of logical calculation—the recognition of a situation, followed by a rational attempt to find a remedy. Mozart did not so much reform opera as transform it, working by instinct in the light of sheer musical and dramatic genius.

Gluck made known his ideas on operatic reform in 1762 with the opera *Orfeo*. Before this date he had been a successful composer of Italian opera in the old style, and a rather less impressive contributor to French opéra comique. The new work revolutionised his career and established him as a composer of fundamental importance. His ideas reflected current intellectual protests at the artificiality of Metastasian operatic conventions (see Chapter IX), and his aim was to produce opera that would express human emotion and realistic drama, rather than pander to the vanity of singers and the stupidity of audiences. Dramatic truth was to be exalted over musical virtuosity.

In a sense, his reforms were negative: he pruned away excesses, but did not always plant new seeds. He cut out complications and improbabilities in the dramatic action, presenting his audience with simple stories in which the interest turned on the psychological growth of the main characters. He simplified the music, removing superfluous ornamentation and cutting down the rigid da capo aria in favour of more flexible structures that could follow the ebb and flow of the dramatic situation. He retained the orchestra to accompany all the recitatives, thus avoiding the slight break in continuity that had always occurred when the harpsichord continuo took over. He made greater use of the chorus, and increased the role of the orchestra.

Gluck gave to opera a sense of dignity and spiritual grandeur—something that had been missing since Monteverdi's day. His 'reformed' operas reflect the quality that the eighteenth century so much admired in Greek and Roman art: 'noble simplicity and calm greatness'.

The olympian nature of Mozart's genius was above conscious reform as such, but the operatic revolution he effected went, in the end, beyond anything Gluck and his associates could have imagined.

Everything the eighteenth century had to offer went into the melting pot of Mozart's genius. His mature operas (*The Marriage of Figaro*, 1786; *Don Giovanni*, 1787; *The Magic Flute*, 1791) draw impartially upon the techniques of opera seria, opera buffa, opéra comique, and singspiel. To this was added his mastery of the symphony and concerto. He was able to weld all these elements into a consistent style, calling upon them individually to whatever extent the dramatic situation demanded. Moreover, he was a dramatist of Shakespearean penetration and subtlety.

Of particular importance is Mozart's development of the ENSEMBLE—the moment when the characters come together to express widely different points of view within a unified musical framework. Here his skill as a symphonist served its turn, transforming what might have been an ingenious formal exercise into a living, constantly developing equivalent of human emotions. Mozart's drama unfolds *through* the music: the music *is* the drama in the deepest possible sense.

So also his arias, drawing on the whole range of form and style, invariably push forward the dramatic action and develop our understanding of the character whose expression they are. Nothing in the Mozart opera merely stands still, to indulge in musical virtuosity for its own sake. Everything has a point and a purpose.

In the same way, the orchestra is made to contribute to the overall dramatic effect. Although it never challenges the supremacy of the voice, it adds its own subtle commentary: sharpening the emotional edges, painting in the background detail, adding in a thousand ways to the unfolding drama. It supports the vocal line, but never degenerates into routine accompaniment.

Above all, Mozart's operas triumph through his sympathy with human nature. He gave life to an enormous range of characters, and followed their fortunes through an equally wide range of emotions and experiences. But like all great dramatists, he created in a spirit of detachment. His characters are not the expression of some personal need of his own, but the outcome of his close observation of human nature. His operas preach no sermons, and strike no moral attitudes—their concern is with nothing so trivial. The Mozart opera holds up a mirror to life itself, wherein all who care to may read.

CHAPTER XV
BEETHOVEN

CALM and ordered though eighteenth century life and art might appear, the seeds of revolution were nourished beneath the surface. The first stirrings are apparent in even so controlled an art as that of Haydn and Mozart. With Beethoven the barriers were down and, as with the French Revolution to which his art was a parallel, the floodtide was released.

Ludwig van Beethoven (1770-1827) was the first composer to regard music as a force that might change the pattern of men's lives. To Beethoven, the master craftsman, craft was only the beginning. Music was a moral force which it was his personal mission to express. He was conscious of greatness, of being set apart from ordinary men, of his duty as a prophet and a leader. Like Napoleon Bonaparte, Beethoven was a man led by a sense of his own destiny—the servant of forces greater than himself.

The typical eighteenth century composer worked in harness. He was employed by a wealthy nobleman to supervise the musical activities of his household: the orchestra, the chamber groups, the opera, the church music. He was expected to compose for each and every occasion. And he was paid, like any servant.

Not every composer enjoyed or accepted these conditions. Mozart, for example, broke away from a particularly offensive employer (the Archbishop of Salzburg), and worked thereafter as a free-lance composer, performer, and teacher. But the rigours and frustrations of a system not yet organised to support any but the wiliest composer eventually killed him.

Beethoven, on the other hand, struck out for independence right from the start. Although willing to satisfy audiences with his playing, and to write, from time to time, music that would please, he made it perfectly clear that he was no man's servant. Rather, he was The Artist—the great man, whose art must be treated as a privilege, a manifestation of Divine Authority. And society, ripe for 'great men'—for Nelsons, Wellingtons, and Napoleons—responded: accepted him at his own valuation and, for the most part, supported him.

Beethoven's example revolutionised the status of the composer. In the past, the composer had supplied a need—sometimes transcending the occasion, sometimes merely satisfying it. From now on they felt themselves to be inspired messengers, bearing gifts that need not be questioned, or even asked for. They felt it essential to prove themselves unique—for Beethoven is the first composer in history to assert that originality was in itself a sign of creative validity.

Although there is scarcely a branch of musical composition that was not, at least in some degree, transformed by his genius, Beethoven's life's work was mainly concerned with the symphony, the concerto, the string quartet, and the piano sonata. His explorations were thus firmly anchored to the sonata principle.

An increase in sheer scale is the first obvious sign of his originality. Beethoven's mature symphonies are much longer than those of Haydn or Mozart. His thematic material is broader and simpler in conception, and its effect is correspondingly massive and powerful. Gone are those vestiges of mid-eighteenth century 'galanterie', which give an air of politeness and grace to even the most impassioned Mozart tune. A Beethoven theme has no time for social graces, it makes its point bluntly and with the maximum force. His was not an art of understatement.

Closely linked with size and breadth of manner is his intense feeling for rhythm. Many of his ideas owe their originality not to any melodic ingenuity, but to their rhythmic force and vitality. Nor is it ever an elusive, subtle rhythm. Beethoven's rhythms are hammered out, and propel his music forward with irresistible strength.

Violence and conflict are at the very core of his style. The abrupt changes of mood to be found in the fashionable 'sturm und drang' (storm and stress) moments in Haydn and Mozart (the musical equivalent of Gothick horror effects), are now part of the general scene—magnified, of course, and almost brutally emphasized. A Beethoven symphony suggests conflict: as if the composer was engaged in subduing the forces of Chaos by a mighty act of Will. It is a measure of his greatness that victory always comes; and it is this that prompts us to equate his most characteristic work with the idea of moral struggle.

The monumental is to be seen everywhere in Beethoven's music. His piano sonatas explore the whole range of the keyboard, leaping from one extreme to the other, gathering in great clusters of notes, changing from sonorous, legato melody to brilliant percussive effects. The comparison with the slender textures and the narrow range of notes in a Mozart or Haydn sonata reflects not only the advance in the structural strength of the piano as an instrument, but, more significantly, the sheer weight and force of Beethoven's style.

In the same way, he made new demands on orchestral instruments, greatly increasing their general range, and extracting from them an altogether more heroic manner of playing. His orchestral style may be less intricate—less imaginative even—than that of his predecessors, but it is infinitely more sonorous and magnificent, and thus admirably suited to the expression of his thought.

It would be misleading to think of Beethoven solely in terms of size and brute force. In certain works, notably the string quartets, he pared down his thought to the point of austerity, thereby achieving a kind of mystical absorption and concentration that is quite unique in music. Equally novel was his tendency to build whole movements from brief thematic fragments—tiny musical seeds that grow with relentless force.

Beethoven's influence upon nineteenth century composers was enormous. Though they did not necessarily try to imitate his style (which would have been foolish, to say the least), consciously or unconsciously they took his achievement as a yardstick with which to measure their own. His mastery of symphonic method elevated the symphony to the position of music's highest goal. His essentially German manner of construction became, for some, the only appropriate mode of thought that serious music could adopt. His insistence on the individuality and uniqueness of the great artist tempted many a lesser man into striking poses he was ill-equipped to maintain. In short: Beethoven's example was both an inspiration and a source of inhibition. He revealed the full potential of music as a means of communication, and thereby set future generations the very real problem of finding something significant to say.

NOTES

NOTES

NOTES

PART FIVE

Romanticism
1827-1900

CHAPTER XVI

THE ROMANTIC MOVEMENT

THE Romantic Movement, which began in English and German literature about the year 1770, found its musical voice during the early part of the nineteenth century. It remained a dominating force in music for nearly a hundred years.

In very broad terms, Romanticism is an attitude of mind that rejects the cool logic of the intellect and trusts instead in the instinctive truths of emotion. Thus, the Romantic Movement represents a reaction against eighteenth century classicism—an Age of Unreason, to counterbalance the Age of Reason.

While Classicism depends upon the conscious mind, Romanticism feeds upon the unconscious. Classicism exalts balance, proportion, moderation, and form. Romanticism revels in emotion, exaggeration, excitement, and fantasy. The Classical artist fulfills his tasks as an ordinary member of society. The Romantic discovers himself in isolation, rejoicing in his solitude.

The way in which Europe developed during the nineteenth century was a stimulus to romanticism and helped to harden its attitudes. Progress, in the shape of industrialization, railways, turbine engines, and all manner of scientific discoveries, rapidly changed the whole structure of society. The rising men were politicians, generals, bankers, and industrialists. Like the sullen masses they controlled, such men had little time for art in any form. Nor had they the inclinations of those earlier patrons, whose leisured nobility and enlightened good taste provided a haven for artistic development. The artist and the moneyed man no longer recognised each other.

In the face of growing materialism, the artist turned away. If he no longer enjoyed an accepted place in society, at least he could justify himself as a self-declared exile, rebel, and prophet of higher things. He struck romantic attitudes—there was little else he could strike.

The artist was thus compelled to deal more and more in terms of himself: exploring his own emotions, and charting the depths of his own personality. He came to regard art as a mirror of the soul. The true artist, he felt, lived for his art, and art existed for its own sake.

Henceforth, the details of the artist's life and personality began to matter enormously. Art was expected to express individuality, uniqueness. It was to be written in the lifeblood of the artist.

This insistence upon individuality can be seen to operate in a larger sense, affecting whole nations.

As the different countries of Europe began to assert their political independence (the nineteenth century is studded with democratic revolution), so also did their artists begin to see a virtue in a national style of art. Previously, such differences had been little more than regional variations upon a basic European theme. Now they were exploited for their own sake, and to a considerable degree.

The fount from which nationalist composers drew their inspiration was, of course, folk music. Untarnished by the sophistications of art, it had remained a natural form of expression for ordinary people. And since it was often based upon primitive scales, and explored wayward rhythms that reflected the peculiar lilt of the language, it fell fresh, and even exotic, on the trained but conventional ears of sensitive composers. What they produced as a result of their studies was a kind of music that can be instantly recognised as belonging to a particular country—a far cry from the universal language of eighteenth century music!

Nationalism blossomed as an effective force in music after the middle of the century and must therefore be considered a characteristic of mature and late Romanticism. The typical interest of the early Romantics was in aspects of the unusual and irrational. As if suddenly distrustful of their own century, artists began to look to distant lands and vanished ages for inspiration. The medieval period, regarded by the eighteenth century as barbaric, now seemed particularly glamorous. Witches, fairies, ghosts, and all the horrid delights of the supernatural claimed serious attention. Commonsense was scarcely able to compete.

The cult of individuality, the exploitation of national styles, the fascination of exotic subjects, all spell out an attitude to art that is essentially personal and inward-looking. The nineteenth century artist turned away from reality to explore his dreams. His greatest achievements are triumphs of imaginative intensity—personal messages from the depths of his experience, eagerly awaited by an audience starved of natural self-expression in the growing materialism of the age.

The relationship between the musician and his audience now began to be played out on quite a different plane from that which had existed in previous centuries. The musician was no longer regarded as an ordinary member of society, doing an ordinary job for ordinary wages. This was not only the age of the 'great' composer, but of the virtuoso performer, and the virtuoso conductor. It also saw the birth of the virtuoso audience, coming together expressly to hear music, as if it were a sacred rite, outside the normal range of experience. So powerful was this new attitude that there now appeared a radical split between popular music (music that could safely be regarded as a useful commodity) and serious music (music that bore the burden of some 'special message'). As an omen, it was not encouraging.

In terms of its actual ingredients, nineteenth century music is remarkable for its consistent exploration of new sounds. An ever-widening range of harmony was admitted into common usage. The ear grew accustomed to dissonance, and more acute forms had to be found in order that discord could make its point at all.

Gradually, as we shall see, this process wore away the very foundations upon which tonal music was built. By the end of the century the carefully graded system of concords and discords, related harmonies and related keys, had all but collapsed. Classical theory no longer supported current practice, and composers were forced to consider what it was that was actually holding their music together and giving it coherence.

This disruption of classical theory came about through nineteenth century determination to make music express ideas and emotions. Over the course of some two hundred years, starting with the birth of opera, a large vocabulary of melodic shapes, expressive harmonies, and colourful orchestral effects had been built up. Because of their original association with words and theatrical situations these devices could be relied upon to trigger off an appropriate emotional response in the listener. The nineteenth century composer turned to this vocabulary in his purely orchestral music. With a little help from words—an apt title, or a programme note—such music could be made to suggest literary and emotional ideas.

PROGRAMME MUSIC of this kind spread rapidly during the century, making its presence felt even in such abstract forms as the symphony. And since it leaned so heavily upon sensation it set composers on a dizzying race for novelty.

As part of the same pattern, the nineteenth century saw great changes in the orchestra and the way in which it was handled. From the middle of the century the orchestra must be thought of as a large body—a hundred players or more, as compared with the twenty-odd of Mozart's day. All are professional musicians, whose sole purpose is to be an orchestra. The instruments they play have been transformed by mechanical inventions into agile, flexible tools. They have been grouped into families of Woodwind, Brass, Percussion, and Strings: all of equal importance and capable of bearing an equal share in the performance.

Moreover, thanks to the example of such composers as Berlioz and Wagner the business of writing for the orchestra now became an art in itself. The composer is no longer content to arrange his music for whatever body of instrumentalists happens to be available. ORCHESTRATION demands that he choose his forces with care, and due regard for the colour they can bring to his music. Once again, it is the search for expressiveness that dominates the scene.

CHAPTER XVII

SYMPHONIC MUSIC IN THE NINETEENTH CENTURY

NINETEENTH century orchestral music can be considered in four main categories: the Symphony, the Symphonic Poem, the Concert Overture, and the Concerto.

The SYMPHONY was largely a German preoccupation, and it is the contributions of German and Austrian composers that form the mainstream of symphonic literature. The procession of great names is impressive: Schubert, Mendelssohn, Schumann, Brahms, Bruckner, Mahler. As for composers outside Germany, with few exceptions their work belonged to the same tradition. Differences of personal temperament, the flavouring of conscious nationalism—such are the minor features we distinguish them by. What binds them together is their debt to Beethoven.

The greater part of nineteenth century symphonic writing

was concerned with the detailed exploration of ground that Beethoven had already uncovered. For example: composers were much occupied by the need for THEMATIC UNITY, wherein all the musical ideas in a symphony were derived from one or two main thematic 'germs' (as in Beethoven's *Fifth*). In the same way, CYCLIC UNITY was much sought after—experiments in binding together the various movements, either by harking back to important themes, or by continual reference to one basic MOTTO THEME.

Following the precedent of Beethoven's *Pastoral Symphony*, overt musical description became an important element in symphonic writing. This, as we shall see, led to a new category: the PROGRAMME SYMPHONY.

Choral additions, as in Beethoven's *Ninth*, also became a feature, bringing the symphony, at times, very close to the cantata in spirit. Words, of course, served to make any message the symphony had to offer all the more explicit.

Less easy to pinpoint, but equally important, is the feeling that, like Beethoven, composers are now personally involved in their music. The weight of a symphony no longer depends on pure musical logic, but on the extent to which it may seem to express the drama of the composer's inner life.

These at least were the ideals of nineteenth century symphonic writing. When it came to the point, most composers were content with an altogether looser approach—making room for picturesque descriptive elements, emotional excursions, theatrical effects. Only Brahms stood out for a wholehearted return to Beethoven's standards.

The characteristic nineteenth century symphony is a symphony with a programme. Sometimes the programme is explicit: the story confirmed in so many words by the composer. Sometimes it is merely implied: felt by the listener to be there, simply because the music is so intense and personal. Either way, there was no escaping the problems of symphonic form. The more a composer wished his music to tell a story, the more necessary it became for him to protect the purely musical logic of his thoughts. It was impossible simply to trust in the story and let the music look after itself.

Both Hector Berlioz (1803-1869) and Franz Liszt (1811-1886), the two great exponents of the PROGRAMME SYMPHONY, evolved systems for ensuring musical coherence. With Berlioz it was the IDÉE FIXE—the obsessional idea that crops up during each movement, as in the *Symphonie Fantastique*, for example, and thus gives a naturally discursive work the necessary feeling of unity.

Liszt's solution was to base all his material on one theme, transforming it as the occasion demanded. He called this working-principle the METAMORPHOSIS OF THEMES. The idea of a MOTTO THEME which recurs at crucial points during each of the four movements is an obvious extension of these innovations.

An important offshoot of the programme symphony was the SYMPHONIC POEM—a large, free form in one movement, intended either to outline a definite story (Strauss's *Don Juan*, for example), or paint pictures and evoke moods (Debussy's *Prélude a l'après-midi d'une Faune*). The actual title 'symphonic poem' is generally credited to Liszt, who was the first to cast a series of works in this mould.

Although, in theory, the form of a symphonic poem depended upon the descriptive task the composer wished to carry out, most composers found it expedient to fit their 'programmes' to some already existing, proven form. Thus Richard Strauss (1864-1949), perhaps the most accomplished composer of programme music, made use of rondo form (*Don Juan*), and theme and variations (*Don Quixote*).

Of the shorter orchestral forms available in the nineteenth century the most important and frequently used was the CONCERT OVERTURE—Mendelssohn's *Hebrides Overture* is an excellent example. Identical in structure with the OPERATIC OVERTURE (a movement in sonata-allegro form), such works were intended solely for the concert platform. More often than not they are also intended as descriptive pieces, and thus have common ground with the symphonic poem.

In some cases a so-called concert overture was in fact an overture that had become divorced from its original function. Beethoven's *Coriolanus Overture*, for example, began life as part of the incidental music to a play. With public concerts on the increase, and the formation of more and more professional orchestras, it was inevitable that the literature of music should be ransacked for suitable material.

Alongside the major orchestral forms there existed two of lesser importance: the SYMPHONIC SUITE, and the set of SYMPHONIC VARIATIONS.

Despite its rather impressive name, the symphonic suite could be almost anything from a collection of movements written as incidental music to a play (Grieg's *Peer Gynt Suite*), a collection of dances from a ballet (Tchaikovsky's *Casse Noisette Suite*), to a series of related, abstract movements that might as easily have been called a symphony. In the one instance the title gave dignity to an attractive rag-bag of pieces, and in the other it enabled the composer to avoid the associations that more explicit titles might have suggested.

Sets of orchestral variations were not widely practised during the period, but the existence of first-rate examples, such as Brahms's *Variations on a theme of Haydn*, makes it a form that cannot be ignored. Sometimes the movements were linked, and therefore flow on in a continuous stream. Invariably the manner of variation was much more symphonic than that of the eighteenth century. The 'theme' is not merely decorated, but used as a source for 'development'.

With the rise of the virtuoso performer and the increase in public concerts, the SOLO CONCERTO inevitably became a popular form with nineteenth century composers. Like the symphony it retained many of its classical features, but there were certain important structural modifications. These include abandoning the 'double exposition' in the first movement—the thematic material is now shared, right from the start; and the removal of the cadenza from its place at the end of the recapitulation, to the more logical and dramatically effective position just before the recapitulation starts. Mendelssohn's delightful *Violin Concerto* shows both these features very clearly.

The Romantic concerto also differs from its Classical prototype in style and manner. Whereas Mozart and his contemporaries had been content with a polite interchange between soloist and orchestra, treating them as partners of equal standing, the Romantic composer thought in terms of virtuosity and technical brilliance. The polite conversation turned, therefore, into a pitched battle—a fight to the death between soloist and orchestra.

Most nineteenth century concertos are either for violin or piano—the two instruments capable of holding their own against fearful odds, and the two most suited to the display of emotional intensity.

Except where it involved the use of a piano, chamber music did not attract the romantics. The string quartet itself was far too severe a medium, far too classical in spirit to allow much room for emotional expression. Those composers who attempted it were often forced into an uneasy quasi-orchestral style which ran counter to the natural genius of the solo instruments. For this reason the combination of strings and piano proved more attractive, the piano lending a greater sonority and breadth of feeling to the occasion.

The masters of chamber music are the same composers who contributed most successfully to the symphony: Schubert, Schumann, Mendelssohn, and, above all, Brahms. But there were few who did not explore its possibilities. It was, after all, an almost obligatory challenge to composers who looked to Beethoven as their guiding light in music.

CHAPTER XVIII

SMALLER FORMS OF THE NINETEENTH CENTURY

THE emphasis the nineteenth century laid upon the miniature forms of piano-piece and art-song may, at first sight, seem in contradiction with the spacious grandeur of its most typical orchestral music. But despite their small scale both lent themselves to an intensely personal kind of expression, and thus had much to offer the Romantic composer.

The chief contributions to the art-song came from Germany, where it flourished under the general title: LIED. During the second half of the century important examples came from France and Russia.

Two factors helped to develop the lied: the rise of German romantic poetry, and the development of the pianoforte.

The piano, invented by Bartolommeo Cristofori about the year 1709, began to come into its own towards the end of the eighteenth century. The roundness of its tone and its poetic, singing qualities delighted the Romantics. They saw in it the ideal partner for the voice—it was almost an orchestra in itself. With their need to express literary ideas in music, the way was open for the creation of art-song.

The first great song writer was Franz Schubert (1797-1828). In more than 600 songs he explored every avenue of approach—from the simple, folk-like melody with an equally simple accompaniment (*Heidenröslein*), to the subtle dramatic song, in which the voice plays an almost operatic role while the piano paints in the background scene and underlines the changes of emotion (*Erlkönig*). As well as separate songs, Schubert also wrote SONG CYCLES: each a collection of songs, bound together by a mood or a story—*Die Winterreise* and *Die Schöne Müllerin*, for example.

The line of great German lieder writers continued after

Schubert through Robert Schumann (1810-1856), Johannes Brahms (1833-1897), and Hugo Wolf (1860-1903). Wolf's contribution is particularly interesting on account of the use he made of Wagnerian techniques (see Chapter XIX)—the main burden of his songs falling to the piano, with the voice adding a realistic, dramatic recitative.

French art-song, generally less dramatic than German and more inclined to sensitive lyricism, grew to greatness in the hands of Henri Duparc (1848-1933), Gabriel Fauré (1845-1924), and Claude Debussy (1862-1918).

Russia produced one outstanding song writer in Modest Moussorgsky (1839-1881), whose songs are remarkable for their dramatic realism. Like Schubert, he explored unusual aspects of human nature, and found beauty in unlikely places.

Although most nineteenth century composers tried their hand at the PIANO SONATA, only Brahms came anywhere near investing the form with the massive significance that Beethoven had brought to it. They were much more at home with short piano pieces, which they could fill with fanciful, poetic ideas the very essence of romanticism.

Such pieces were either free in form, or relatively simple in construction. Dance patterns were enormously popular: the WALTZ, the MAZURKA, the POLONAISE. And so were evocative titles, such as ROMANZA, BALLADE, NOCTURNE, FANTASY, and IMPROMPTU. Some pieces deliberately exploited various aspects of keyboard technique—the ETUDE, for example.

The great genius of piano music was Frédéric Chopin (1810-1849), an archetype Romantic, pouring out his soul in rapturous self-communion. In his hands the piano developed a singing quality that was operatic in its intensity. He explored an extraordinary range of pianistic devices, transmuting them, however, from exercises in mere technique into powerful statements of a highly developed imagination. At the same time he also made outstanding contributions to the development of harmony—far outstripping, in daring, most composers of his day.

If Chopin symbolized the fiery aspirations of Polish nationalism, Schumann, his contemporary and equally a poet of the keyboard, spoke for the quieter, domestic virtues of the nineteenth century. He too explored the smaller forms, but linked them with ideas that were sometimes literary and sometimes intimately personal. A true Romantic, music for him was very much a matter of autobiography.

The easier songs and piano pieces were bought in vast quantities by middle-class amateurs. Home music-making became a feature of nineteenth century life, and together with concert-going and choral singing, it represents a distinct move towards the democratization of good music. From now on, such delights were no longer the perogative of the rich.

An outstanding example of this popularization can be seen in the spread of choral singing. In England and Germany singing was regarded as a healthy recreation for the masses. Attempts were made to find simple ways of teaching musical notation—the Tonic-sol-fa system, for example, dates from the 1840's. Choral Societies sprang up in every town, and Choral Festivals became the order of the day. And when music publishers, led by the London firm of Novellos, began to issue the standard classics in cheap editions, the last barriers were cleared away.

Choral singing was essentially a middle-class movement, and was thus mainly concerned with easily acceptable styles in music. The 'advanced' composer cut very little ice in these circles. Typical of the period was the ORATORIO: rooted firmly in the traditions of Handel, orthodox in its Old Testament subject matter, conservative in its musical content. Felix Mendelssohn (1805-1847) was its most successful exponent.

Even Catholic composers were drawn into the oratorio market. Liszt, Dvořák, Gounod and Elgar, all made important contributions—as did such free-thinkers as Berlioz.

Significant settings of the mass and requiem continued to be made, but they were mostly written for the concert hall. Beethoven's *Missa Solemnis,* Brahms's *German Requiem,* the requiems of Berlioz, Verdi and Fauré, are all works that call for a large, professional chorus, fine soloists, and an accomplished orchestra. They express the composer's personal attitude to Christianity rather than seek to interpret the liturgy in traditional terms. They are thus typical of the Romantic period.

CHAPTER XIX
NINETEENTH CENTURY OPERA

AT the turn of the century the focal point of operatic interest moved, very briefly, from Italy to France. Encouraged by the momentous events of the Revolution, French composers (or,

Nineteenth-century harmony: Wagner *Tristan und Isolde* (Prelude)
Continuous modulation; discord melting into discord; yearning, short-breathed melodic phrases—all contribute to the undermining of classical tonality.

Reprinted by permission of Durand & Cie, Paris

Twentieth-century freedom: Debussy *Preludes* (No 10 from Book 2)
A stream of parallel chords; unexpected harmonic juxtapositions; moments of bitonality; flexible, wayward melodic shapes—these are some of the elements that contribute to the tonal freedom of the twentieth century.

more accurately, composers who happened to be working in Paris) began to develop a type of spectacular opera that dealt in last-minute rescues, elaborate crowd scenes, historical backgrounds, and strong melodramatic climaxes.

Beginning in a reasonably controlled fashion in the work of Luigi Cherubini (1760-1842) and Gaspare Spontini (1774-1851), GRAND OPERA, as it was called, reached its most extravagant expression with Giacomo Meyerbeer (1791-1864).

Sensation and spectacle accounted for nearly everything in grand opera. Yet it would be wrong to dismiss it as nothing more than a pile of indescriminate climaxes. At its best it could be forceful and true to human emotions. And its influence was strong enough to embrace such diverse talents as Rossini, Verdi, and Wagner.

Alongside French grand opera ran the less pretentious stream of OPÉRA COMIQUE, ministered to by such composers as: François Boieldieu (1775-1834), Daniel Auber (1782-1871), and Louis Hérold (1791-1833). This developed in two directions: into the pure entertainment of OPERETTA, as exemplified in the works of Jacques Offenbach (1819-1880); and into the more serious, sentimental style known as LYRIC OPERA, as represented by Charles Gounod (1818-1893), Ambroise Thomas (1811-1896), and Jules Massenet (1842-1912).

Slightly to one side of the generally accepted operatic styles is the figure of Hector Berlioz, whose masterpiece *The Trojans* managed to contain full-blooded romanticism within a classical framework that is reminiscent of Lully, Rameau, and Gluck. This isolated and unique opera had no immediate influence—its true stature was only realised in the twentieth century. Something of the same isolation surrounds Debussy's only operatic venture, *Pélleas et Mélisande* (1902)—again, a masterpiece.

Towards the end of the nineteenth century a further influence came from France in the shape of Bizet's *Carmen* (1875). This took as its subject matter a realistic, low-life story, which it treated with appropriate directness. Later Italian composers (Mascagni, and Puccini) were to exploit this vein under the banner of VERISMO.

The traditions of Italian opera developed in an unbroken line from the eighteenth to nineteenth centuries, with Gioacchino Rossini (1792-1868) as the bridge between them. Rossini's work stretches from opera seria and opera buffa on the one hand, to his final experiments in grand opera (*William Tell*, 1829) on the other. He was followed by two composers who explored a more lyrical style—a kind of domestic grand opera, in which romantic, sentimental plots were decked out with the minimum of orchestral accompaniment and the maximum of sensuous, virtuoso *bel canto*. Both Vincenzo Bellini (1801-1835) and Gaetano Donizetti (1797-1848) pressed the emotional possibilities of fine singing to the uttermost.

The commanding figure in Italian opera is Giuseppi Verdi (1813-1901), whose life work drew together the different strands of French and Italian opera in a distinctive personal style which may aptly be called HEROIC OPERA.

The strength of Verdi's utterance lay in his command over soaring vocal melody—crude and forceful in his early operas (*Nabucco, Ernani*, etc), subtle and infinitely varied in his final masterpieces (*Aida, Otello, Falstaff*). During the course of a long creative life his treatment of the orchestra grew from mere accompaniment to an integral commentary upon the drama and emotions he wished to portray. But he never allowed it to challenge the ultimate supremacy of the human voice.

Although Verdi's operas follow the nineteenth century tendency to blurr over the distinction between aria and recitative, his arias remained recognisably arias, and his ensembles formal set-pieces. Yet he was able to weld an apparently artificial set of conventions into profound musical drama, wherein each art respects the other's genius and thereby achieves an amalgam that is greater than both.

During his lifetime Verdi became, for Italians struggling towards political unity and freedom from Austrian domination, a symbol of national aspiration. Consciously, he shaped his operas so as to reflect the longings of his fellow countrymen. Unconsciously, the vigour of his style reflected the heroic nature of their struggle to gain freedom and self respect.

Operatic developments in Germany proceeded along very different lines from those in either France or Italy. At the beginning of the century German opera was dominated by a sense of nationalism. Based in part upon the traditions of singspiel (see Chapter XIV) there sprang up a style of ROMANTIC OPERA that made use of German folk-lore, and fused conventional operatic methods with simple, folk-like melodies. Typical of their period, these operas took a great delight in supernatural subjects, the romantic beauties of nature, and the virtues of peasant life. The most important composer of such operas was Carl Maria von Weber (1786-1826), whose masterpiece was *Der Freischütz*. He was followed, rather lamely, by Heinrich Marschner (1795-1861).

Even in these early stages German opera was inclined to make more use of the orchestra than the Italians, and it is this tendency that eventually emerged as the fundamental difference between the two national styles. With Richard Wagner (1813-1883), German opera became frankly symphonic.

Wagner's starting point was a mixture of German romantic opera and French grand opera, but he rapidly developed views of his own on the true nature of music and the theatre. He aimed at an operatic revolution which would overthrow artificial conventions and replace them with a work in which music, poetry, and stagecraft would be united in a new dramatic truth. He dropped the word 'opera' and began to call his work: MUSIC DRAMA.

Like Verdi, Wagner was a convinced nationalist. His contribution to the struggle for German unification was to be the creation of a national, heroic myth, which would demonstrate Aryan virtues once and for all. He wrote his own libretti, drawing upon three major themes: German folk-lore and mythology; a romantic view of medieval life; and the idea of redemption through love (a fleshly parallel to the Christian message). His mature works—the *Ring* cycle (*Das Rheingold, Die Walküre, Siegfried, Götterdämmerung*), *Tristan und Isolde, Die Meistersinger von Nürnburg*, and *Parsifal*—deal, in varying degrees, with these three main issues.

The visionary nature of Wagner's ideas, together with his astonishing ability to render them in practical terms, conspired with nationalist fervour to surround his music dramas in an almost religious aura. This was no mere theatrical entertainment, but a solemn ceremony demanding the devotion of unquestioning disciples. As a fit temple for his art he was eventually able to build his own Festival Theatre at Bayreuth (1876), where meticulous attention to detail set a new and highly influential standard for theatrical production throughout Europe.

The structure of Wagner's music dramas is equally revolutionary. To achieve a sense of dramatic continuity he abandoned the aria and recitative formula altogether. In its place he put a continuous orchestral background, built up symphonically, against which the voices might sing in an expressive arioso style. The many different themes that were woven into his orchestral textures he called LEITMOTIVS. Each stood for a particular person, object, or idea in the drama, and could be developed according to the dramatic needs of the moment. The similarity between this approach and the methods of Liszt and Berlioz in their programme music (see Chapter XVIII) is obvious.

The main burden of explaining the drama thus fell to the orchestra. Despite his theories about artistic 'equality', the voice took second place, becoming, in effect, an additional orchestral instrument. The task of unfolding the drama along symphonic lines inevitably led to an increase in sheer length. The Wagner music drama takes twice and three times as long to explain itself as conventional opera.

Everything about Wagner and his works was monumental. The length of his music dramas, the size of the orchestra they required, the strain they put on the singing voice—everything was in excess of anything that had been known. In his personal life he was the Romantic Artist, *par excellence*. Dedicated, aloof, selfish, scornful; driven by his daemon to struggle against fearful odds; ultimately victorious—there had been nothing like it since Beethoven. And like Beethoven he left a very long shadow.

So far as the materials of music are concerned, Wagner's importance lies in the lengths to which he stretched the principles of harmony and modulation which had been the basis of music since the middle of the seventeenth century. In order to pursue an effect of yearning, ecstatic emotion (*Tristan und Isolde*, for example), he turned increasingly to dissonance. His discords no longer resolved smoothly and promptly into acceptable concords. Instead, they melted into further discords, perpetually delaying the ultimate resolution.

Though powerfully expressive, these techniques began to undermine the feeling of tonality upon which they depended. Discords were felt not so much as deviations from an obvious concord, but as colours in their own right. Modulation as a means of building up a musical structure began to fail, because the music was always modulating.

In Wagner's hands the old terms of reference just hold. But the attempt to go further could only lead, as we shall see, to a collapse of the whole system.

Two minor schools of National Opera are important. From Bohemia came a series of works by Bedřich Smetana (1824-1884) and Antonín Dvořák (1841-1904), based on Czech legends and folk-lore and making use of national dance rhythms. Beneath the national flavouring, however, is a basically German style.

From Russia, on the other hand, came something more individual. Russian music awoke to effective consciousness with the operas of Michael Glinka (1804-1857), emerging in full force with the work of Modest Mussorgsky (1839-1881), Alexander Borodin (1833-1887), and Nicholas Rimsky-korsakov (1844-1908).

Tchaikovsky's operas, like his orchestral music, cannot be

said to be truly nationalistic. They are, rather, a blend of French and German romanticism, and, as such, remarkably successful.

The kind of subject-matter to which nineteenth century opera turned its attention was altogether more 'meaty' than that which had appealed to previous centuries. Its aim was to please a middle-class audience, which liked to have its emotions swayed and its sense of theatrical magic aroused. As in the concert hall, the process of musical democratization was at work.

NOTES

NOTES

NOTES

PART SIX

Modern
1900 onwards

CHAPTER XX

THE PROBLEMS OF TWENTIETH CENTURY MUSIC

THE closer we are to events, the more difficult they become to understand. We can view the distant past with detachment, confident that time has already sifted much of the information we wish to interpret. But the present is too personal a concern; and so, for the most part, is the immediate past. Try as we may, we cannot see them in perspective.

Any attempt to explain the music of the twentieth century can therefore only hope to trace the most obvious outlines. And we must be prepared to see even these change in the light of future events.

There is scarcely any aspect of human thought and activity that has not undergone radical changes in the last fifty years. Ideas and attitudes that once seemed impregnable have now been either discarded or fundamentally reconsidered. The extraordinary advances in scientific discovery have not only changed the conditions of man's existence, but also his understanding of himself. In an age which deals in terms of atomic power, instant radio and telecommunications, interplanetary travel, an infinite universe, and a host of similar wonders, the traditional conception of man's role on earth has had to be revised.

Such far-reaching changes would have been confusing under any circumstances. But they have been brought about with such speed that the average man can scarcely absorb or even acknowledge them. Add to this the cataclysmic effects of two World Wars, and the prospect of a third which may even succeed in wiping out the whole of civilisation, and it is easy to see why the picture of present-day life is bewildering.

Contemporary arts not only reflect the general confusion and uncertainty, but have also been subject to revolutions of their own. So far as music is concerned, the twentieth century represents a period of change comparable only to the transition from modal polyphony to diatonic harmony at the beginning of the seventeenth century. Composers have scarcely begun to map out the new tonal landscape that now confronts them.

By the end of the nineteenth century the principles governing the music that Europe had developed over a period of some three hundred years (tonal music) had virtually ceased to apply to the kind of music that many composers found themselves writing. The seeds of crisis can be seen in the work of Richard Wagner: constant modulation, a high degree of chromatic inflection within the diatonic scale, and a vast rise in the number of permitted discords. The music of such composers as Max Reger, Richard Strauss, and the young Arnold Schönberg, developed this line of thought still further.

Long before the First World War it was generally accepted that the laws of tonality were not, after all, divine and incontrovertible. Obviously something had to be done. To some composers the problem and its answer were clear-cut: if tonality no longer held good, then its opposite, ATONALITY, must. To others, whose inheritance was either non-European (like Bartók and Stravinsky), or less committed to the German classics (like Debussy), the solution was less easy to define, but it involved moving forward to a state of what may best be called FREE TONALITY.

Either way, the result was a very different kind of music from that which had satisfied previous generations. To understand it the music-lover had to drop old expectations of what was right and proper, and listen as it were with new ears. Needless to say, not all of them were prepared to make the effort. The tendency to worship the heritage of the past now increased, and twentieth century music-making rapidly split into a museum of cherished classics on the one hand, and a rather belligerent *avant garde* on the other. For the first time in musical history, innovation began to be cultivated as an end in itself.

The new music differed in other respects also. Late nineteenth century composers had left a legacy of large-scale works, sumptuously scored for gigantic orchestras, and calling upon the extremes of emotional effect. For all its splendour it was a kind of music that could seem too rich to be healthy—like fruit, so ripe that it can only turn bad.

The most influential twentieth century composers reacted against the over-heated romanticism of their predecessors. Instead, they cultivated a deliberately cool music that went out of its way to avoid emotional excess (or even any kind of emotion), that made a virtue out of scientific detachment. They turned from lengthy works to short pieces, from large orchestras to chamber groups, from high-flown rhetoric to understatement.

The ground-plan for the development of music in the twentieth century can best be approached through the work of five major composers: Debussy, Schönberg, Bartók, Hindemith, and Stravinsky. Between them they encompass the problems of excessive romanticism, anti-romanticism, atonality, and free tonality—not to mention the many 'isms' that critics have introduced as labels to explain passing developments as they occurred.

Their work, of course, was paralleled by the efforts of many lesser composers. However much their experiments may have been crowned with the final authority of genius, they did not work in glorious isolation. The crisis concerned everybody.

CHAPTER XXI

EXPERIMENTS IN TONALITY

IT is only in recent years that musicians have come to recognise the importance of the revolution brought about by Claude Debussy (1862-1918). Unlike the atonal composers of Vienna, he formulated no special theory to account for his music, and left behind him no ardent disciples intent on preaching the gospel of his methods. He wrote instinctively and to please himself, but in doing so demonstrated that there were ways of approaching music that were quite different from those built up by the great German masters from Bach to Wagner.

If Debussy had any thought of conscious revolution it was simply to throw off German musical domination—that of Wagner in particular. Much as he might admire Wagner's genius, he was not interested in his methods.

What did interest him, however, were the wayward, unclassical scales of folk music and oriental cultures (primitive scales, such as the five-note [pentatonic] scale, and the seven-note whole-tone scale). Tunes cast in these moulds simply did not fit the classical system of harmony. Yet the tunes themselves were not at fault.

All they needed was a different kind of harmonic approach—one that Debussy's sensitive instincts were able to discover.

The classical melody—the Bach-Beethoven-Wagner variety—throws a very strong harmonic shadow. It is balanced on a series of formal cadences, and calls into existence an orthodox sequence of chords. It is a melody conceived in terms of an underlying harmonic progression, and the tonality that this implies.

But classical melody is not the only type of melody. It is merely the melody of a particular period. The melodies of modal music, as we have seen, were quite different. So also are the melodies of folk and oriental cultures. Instead of being held together by the tonality of an implied harmony, these melodies hover round certain important notes, which themselves assume the function of tonics—that is: fixed points of reference. This method of organisation may conveniently be called MELODIC TONALITY.

Debussy was attracted to existing melodies of this kind, and naturally inclined to invent examples of his own. It is perhaps worth noting that the only major classical-romantic composer to think along somewhat similar lines, Hector Berlioz, was also a Frenchman. French music has always stood a little apart from the German manner.

Since classical harmonies could not be made to fit his melodies, Debussy was forced to discover harmonic methods of his own. Sustained chords, animated by a swirl of figuration, held as a background against which the melody floats, sometimes in tune with the harmony, sometimes not, is one method he employed. Chords moving in parallel with the melody—a kind of modern organum—was another. A third approach produced the equivalent of a harmonic patchwork quilt, with chords in juxtaposition rather than progression. It was all a matter of inate musical taste—and Debussy's taste was inspired by genius.

The result of his experiments was to release European music from the straight-jacket of German classical-romantic harmony. Tonality was not abandoned, but simply given a new freedom and flexibility. The old harmonies were preserved, but no longer obliged to obey the laws of fixed progression. Melody could now assert its independence, deriving just as much support from the harmony as it needed.

Much of Debussy's music is made effective by his extraordinarily sensitive choice of orchestral colour. Unlike the German romanticists, who tended to think in terms of structural lines weaving together through the orchestra, Debussy's music is conceived in delicate washes of sound. The actual notes his instruments play may have very little structural significance, but the atmosphere they create is all-important. Excellent examples of these techniques can be seen in the *Prélude a l'après midi d'une Faune,* 1894; *Nocturnes,* 1895; *La Mer,* 1905; and *Images pour orchestre,* 1909.

The particular quality of delicate, shimmering sound patterns in Debussy's music led many people to draw a parallel with the IMPRESSIONIST school of painting (Monet, Manet, Degas, Renoir, Pissaro). They detected what they took to be the same vagueness of outline, the same reliance on atmosphere and palpitating colour. Though there is some truth in the idea, it has, unfortunately, tended to divert attention from the true nature of his innovations. He was, as critics now realise, something more than a hedonistic reveller in sensuous sound.

Having achieved harmonic and melodic freedom through the music of Debussy, the twentieth century went on to explore rhythmic freedom through the experiments of Béla Bartók (1881-1945), and Igor Stravinsky (1882-1971).

Stravinsky, the Russian, and Bartók, the Hungarian, received their earliest musical impressions in countries outside the main influence of German traditions. Folk music was a living force in their countries—not merely something preserved in a museum—and they were later able to use its lessons in freeing their own music from classical preconceptions (Debussy's example, of course, showed them the way). But they were also affected by the free rhythms of folk music, and these became an added source of inspiration and originality.

Classical music deals in symmetrical rhythms, spelled out in a series of regular accents arranged in groups of two or three beats (or multiples thereof). Very occasionally irregular patterns were introduced (fives, or sevens), but once set up, even these tended to be maintained in a regular fashion.

Against this steady, dance-like pulse, classical composers allowed themselves counter-accents (SYNCOPATION), and a considerable rhythmic variety between different parts in a texture (a legacy of true polyphony). But the basic pulse was always in itself as regular as clockwork.

Stravinsky and Bartók introduced the idea of asymmetrical rhythm into European music. The beats were there, strong and obvious, but they followed a fluctuating and unpredictable pattern. Sometimes this involved changing the time-signature with almost every bar. Sometimes it involved using different time-signatures in different parts—a bass moving in threes, against a melody moving in twos, for example. Thus, as with

Debussy's harmony, an old tradition was enriched and revitalized.

The experiments of Debussy, Stravinsky, and Bartók, prepared what may be called the *basic* style of twentieth century music. Without precisely imitating them, other composers were able to proceed along similar lines with equally fruitful results. Audiences, though sometimes startled by unexpected effects, have found it fairly easy to accept the new music as a logical extension of old methods.

Despite the claims of its adherents, and the undeniable fact that it too can trace a logical path of development from traditional methods, the same degree of general acceptance has not yet been given to ATONAL music.

The concept of atonality was propounded by Arnold Schönberg (1874-1951), and explored by his friends Anton Webern (1883-1945) and Alban Berg (1885-1935). All three were born in Vienna, in the heart of the classical tradition.

Schönberg's early work, up to about 1908, was strongly romantic and Wagnerian. Like Debussy, however, he too came to realise that Wagner had strained classical principles to breaking point, but his Germanic outlook insisted that some new *theory* would have to be called in to explain the logic of the music his instincts prompted him to write.

Although from 1909 his music was, to all intents and purposes, atonal—that is to say: the harmonies appear to have no logical connecting links, the melodies are angular, disjointed and highly chromatic, discords exist freely and without acknowledging any obligation to seek a satisfactory resolution in concords, and, above all, there is no over-riding sense of key—it was not until 1921 that Schönberg declared what it was he believed he had discovered.

He decided, from a study of his own music, that all twelve notes of the chromatic scale were of equal importance. There were no longer any focal points (tonics and dominants) around which all the other notes gravitated. The twelve notes were independent of each other, except when organised into significant melodic patterns.

It therefore seemed essential that if this aspect of equality was to be maintained, no one note ought to be repeated more frequently than any other. If one note should recur in this insistent fashion, it would inevitably assume the role of a tonic and begin to dominate the situation.

Schönberg's answer, known as the TWELVE NOTE SYSTEM, or SERIAL TECHNIQUE, is a suggestion for arriving at pure atonality. The twelve-note composition is based on a melodic series consisting of the twelve notes of the chromatic scale, arranged in any order, but not necessarily keeping to the limits of one octave. This series provides the thematic material for the composition, and also stands in lieu of the traditional scale—that is: it establishes a basic order of events.

To preserve the equality of the twelve notes, no note in the series is repeated in a given part until all twelve notes have appeared—either horizontally, as a melody, or vertically, grouped together as chords.

The tone row is open to every variety of rhythmic change, and this, of course, provides endless opportunities for disguise and variation. Like an ordinary tune, it may be turned upside down, used back-to-front, or both upside down and back-to-front. The entire row may be transposed to higher or lower pitches. What matters is that the series of twelve notes should revolve throughout the composition, maintaining a strict relationship. Turning it upside down, and so on, does not alter the internal relationships—it is merely as if the row were a physical object being looked at from different angles.

In the early days of twelve-note composition many composers went out of their way to avoid any combination of notes that might suggest the simple chords of tonal music. They also held strictly to their tone rows. As they grew more practised in their art and more confident, however, they felt able to relax this vigilence and even produced music that has strong tonal affinities.

One of the attractions of serial technique lies in the integrity it imposes on each aspect of a composition. Since everything flows from the tone row, everything is accounted for and has a logical explanation. In a period that was reacting against excessive, wayward romanticism, this kind of intellectual consistency had a very strong appeal to certain composers.

Having overthrown tonality, serial composers were forced, by sheer logic, to avoid certain other features associated with it. They began to shun obvious 'themes', obvious formal patterns, obvious rhythmic pulses—everything, in fact, that might remind the listener of tonality and its methods. In doing this they were not behaving wilfully, but merely taking proper precautions. Their music was to be listened to with new ears: far better, then, that the listener should not be confused with reminiscences of the past.

An extreme example of this new style can be seen in the music of Webern, whose brief, highly concentrated pieces could scarcely be more different from the lush, long-winded efforts of the late romantics. In his work short phrases and individual notes are given a new significance by being made to appear in isolation. This kind of fragmentation was to have an enormous influence on music after the second World War.

One further attempt to provide a theoretical explanation for the way in which modern music was behaving deserves notice. It was provided by Paul Hindemith (1895-1963), who evolved a theory of harmonic relationships in which any combination of the twelve chromatic notes could be shown to have a certain fixed value in relation to a tonal centre.

The attraction of Hindemith's system was that it is based firmly on the natural acoustic properties of music. He observed that when one note is sounded it contains also a host of lesser notes—its OVERTONE series. These help to give it its character and roundness. First in the series comes the octave, and then the fifth—and so on, until all twelve semitones have been accounted for. Obviously the strength of a relationship between consecutive notes must depend upon their relationship to each other in the overtone series. From this observation Hindemith was able to suggest a system governing the relationship of every conceivable degree of concord and discord.

Despite its manifest attractions, Hindemith's proposals have never caught on to quite the extent that might have been predicted. They are respected, but largely ignored—or, at least, not much talked about.

CHAPTER XXII

CHANGING STYLES IN THE TWENTIETH CENTURY

THE common factors shared by all significant twentieth century music are, as we have seen, the abandonment of classical tonality, and the revolt against excessive romanticism. This revolutionary change of attitude has not been easy to achieve. Along the way many experiments have been tried: some of permanent value, some reflecting only a passing fashion. But such is the nature of our society that all of them have been eagerly seized upon, labelled and duly advertized. The result is a bewildering maze of musical signposts, often pointing to side-issues that lead only to dead ends.

Yet it is precisely these explorations that make up the history of twentieth century music. Though none of them have produced the final, all-embracing solution to the problem of creating a new style, they have all made useful contributions. And all of them have been steps along the broad road to free tonality.

The label attached to that sizeable body of music which continued to explore late nineteenth century German traditions is NEO-ROMANTICISM. Such music, associated mainly with opera, symphony, concerto and symphonic poem, was still being composed well into the twentieth century, in the teeth of new developments, and often with great success. The most outstanding contributions came from Richard Strauss, Gustav Mahler (1860-1911), Edward Elgar (1857-1934), Jean Sibelius (1865-1957), Carl Nielsen (1865-1931), and Serge Rachmaninov (1873-1943). Their music—large-scale, emotional, and scored for vast orchestras—inevitably seems like the long sunset of a dying tradition.

IMPRESSIONISM, the term wished primarily upon Debussy's music, aroused the interest of other composers. Its influence can be seen quite strongly in Maurice Ravel (1875-1937), Frederick Delius (1862-1934), Manuel de Falla (1876-1946), and to a lesser degree in Ralph Vaughan Williams (1872-1958), Giacomo Puccini (1858-1924), and Béla Bartók.

Another term borrowed from painting was EXPRESSIONISM. This was applied to music that set out to explore extreme emotional states, particularly those associated with the subconscious mind. The connection with the discoveries of psychoanalysis, itself a twentieth century toy, is obvious. Expressionist music is always extremely dissonant, angular in melody, and dislocated in its rhythms. The operas of Richard Strauss (*Salomé* and *Elektra*), and Alban Berg (*Wozzeck* and *Lulu*), provide, along with various semi-theatrical works of Schönberg, good examples of the genre.

NATIONALISM continued to play an important part in twentieth century music, and in certain instances its effects were far-reaching. Whereas earlier composers had tended merely to dabble in folk music, treating it as a source of exotic effects that might be applied, like a cosmetic, to a basically European style, the new nationalist-composer approached it with much greater reverence. He collected his material with scrupulous care (the newly-invented gramophone was a great boon), studied it in depth, and absorbed its essential spirit into his music. Snatches of folksong no longer drift like undigested foreign bodies in the texture of concert works, but are part and parcel of the whole manner of composition.

The effect of folksong studies, as we have already noticed, was often to introduce composers to unusual scales, strange harmonic progressions, and irregular rhythms—all of which helped them not only to find a style of their own and a style for their country, but to combat the inhibiting influence of an exhausted and dying tonal tradition. Such composers as Béla Bartók and Zoltán Kodály (1882-1966) in Hungary, Leoš Janáček (1858-1926) in Czechoslovakia, and Gustav Holst (1874-1934) and Ralph Vaughan Williams in England, all found their way to free tonality through the paths of folk music.

Perhaps the most advertised of twentieth century '-isms' was NEO-CLASSICISM. This movement, centred largely on Paris and the work of Igor Stravinsky and the group of French composers known as 'Les Six', of whom Darius Milhaud (1892-1974) and Francis Poulenc (1899-1963) were the most important, was inspired by a revulsion against excessive romanticism. It aimed at reproducing the ideals of the eighteenth century through the resources of modern harmony, melody and rhythm.

Neo-classic composers often borrowed old formal patterns (such as the minuet, the da capo aria, the concerto grosso) and old melodic habits, but added new and unexpected twists. A melody that began like Mozart would suddenly be tweaked out of shape. Classical dance rhythms would miss a beat and go tumbling. Harmonies would be pushed askew to produce a deliberately 'wrong note' effect.

Such devices resulted in a kind of music that is sophisticated, witty, and elegant, slightly mocking, and utterly unsentimental. Its textures are simple and uncluttered, its harmonies astringent, and its formal patterns clearly outlined. Counterpoint, often presented in a 'Back to Bach' spirit, is a frequent ingredient. It did much to explode the nineteenth century belief that the great artist must strive only after great emotions if he is to be at all worth listening to.

In view of the attitude of mind involved, it is not surprising to find that it was neo-classical composers who were largely responsible for the introduction of American JAZZ techniques into 'serious' music. Jazz had developed into a popular art form during the first decades of the century. In contrast to the often pretentious formalities of concert music, it seemed to sum up everything that was lively and forward-looking It therefore had a immediate appeal to bright young composers engaged in kicking off the dead weight of tradition.

Successful examples of jazz-inspired 'serious' music are to be found in the work of Stravinsky (*L'Histoire du Soldat*), Milhaud (*La Création du Monde*), and in the stage works of Kurt Weill (1900-1950). In the long run, however, serious music borrowed comparatively little from jazz—if anything, the traffic has flowed in the other direction.

Although we have associated certain names with the different explorations so far dealt with, this has been more a matter of convenience than pigeon-holed fact. Almost all the great composers of the twentieth century have had a share in more than one of the exploratory avenues, and some have ventured in each of them. The extreme example of this enterprising spirit is, of course, Stravinsky—who began his career as a romantic impressionist, and passed through the whole gamut of 'isms', to end up, in his old age, in the clear light of atonality.

In the same way, within these different avenues of approach there are many common aspects of style.

For example: the breakdown of the tonal system led composers to explore the problem of combining notes into acceptable harmonies. New scale systems were introduced—pentatonic, whole-tone, and quasi-oriental scales. Chords and melodies constructed from material of this kind were bound to contradict the conventions of diatonic music.

Some composers turned again to the old church modes, adding their peculiar flavour to modern techniques (Vaughan Williams, for example, was deeply indebted to them). A few even went so far as to divide the octave into more than twelve steps, thus producing the quarter-tones and micro-tones of Eastern music.

Experiments in harmony and harmonic progression include: DISPLACED TONALITY, where sections of music in remotely related keys are introduced one after the other, usually without any linking modulation. This effect of abrupt JUXTAPOSITION has become very much part of the twentieth century musical scene. It is, of course, the complete opposite of the classical art of smooth TRANSITION. The modern mind appears to enjoy leaping about in this way—similar techniques are to be found in films, radio, and even books. Step-by-step connecting links are no longer thought necessary.

Music in which different strands, either of melody or block harmony, are clearly in two different keys is said to be BITONAL. If more than two keys are involved the result is POLYTONALITY. Most twentieth century composers have exploited this effect—usually in small doses. Good examples can be seen in the work of Stravinsky, Bartók, Milhaud, and Vaughan Williams.

Deliberate bitonality has been particularly valuable in helping composers reach what is perhaps the basic condition of modern music: the treatment of the different parts of a texture as if each existed on a plane of its own. Music IN PERSPECTIVE, in fact.

All the elements in classical music (melody, bass-line, harmony, and rhythm) exist in the same plane. The harmony springs out of the bass-line, the melody rises out of the movement of the harmonies and is articulated by the rhythmic pulse. Each is dependent on the other, for they are all aspects of the same thought and cannot be divided.

Not so in twentieth century music. Here the harmony may exist in its own stream, forming a background against which a largely independent melody is projected. The rhythm of the harmony may be quite different from that of the melody. A percussion part may add a rhythm that has nothing to do with either. Each element occupies its own layer of existence, like different strata in a rock face. The result is a form of counterpoint, to be listened to 'in perspective'.

It goes without saying that the effectiveness of this approach can depend very much on the instrumental colours involved. The feeling of background and foreground can be heightened by this means, thus providing a guide which tells the ear how to listen. Orchestration is an integral part of twentieth century composition.

CHAPTER XXIII

THE MUSIC OF THE TWENTIETH CENTURY

IN the absence of an agreed musical language each twentieth century composer has been forced to choose, or invent, a style for himself. Far from acting as a brake upon composition, the predicament seems to have been a positive stimulus to creative activity. Probably more music has been written in this century than in any other. Certainly there are far more composers.

The richness and variety of music has also been greatly increased, not only because each country has tended to produce styles in line with its own traditions and personality, but because the cult of individual expression, carried over from nineteenth century romanticism, is still very much in evidence. Moreover, since ideas can now be communicated with the greatest ease, the composer has been able to draw inspiration from a vast number of sources. He may be as stimulated by the music of India or Java as by the folksongs of his own country. He may find the techniques of Dufay and Dunstable as worthy of imitation as those of his own contemporaries. The twentieth century has taken up the inheritance of the whole world and the entire known past.

It is therefore no surprise to find old formal patterns, such as the concerto grosso, flourishing merrily alongside recent innovations—often within the same composition. The modern composer feels at liberty to use whatever ingredients best suit his needs. And this, of course, is why it is so difficult to define twentieth century style.

The main preoccupations have been, as before: the symphony and concerto, chamber music, opera, solo song, and choral music. Most composers have made interesting contributions in all these forms; and they have appeared in every possible style.

In handling symphonic forms most composers have acknowledged the practical effectiveness of at least some version of the sonata-allegro structure. It is usually no longer possible to speak of Exposition, Development and Recapitulation sections, or of any orthodox key scheme. The old patterns are there, but made infinitely fluid and subtle.

The most important general tendency has been to avoid the use of full-blown first and second subjects, or any kind of formal exposition. Movements are more often evolved from a number of basic 'germ' themes—the accent being on 'motivic consistency'. This desire to account for everything is, of course, part of the general reaction against wayward romanticism. It has been much encouraged by the intellectual rigours of serial technique.

Probably the most important developments along these lines are to be seen in the symphonies of Jean Sibelius. In his mature works the movements are built up almost visibly—starting with meaningless thematic scraps that gradually combine or react with each other so as to develop into an extended statement. Sometimes this principle is carried out over several movements, so that the finale comes as a grand summing-up of everything that has gone before. A logical extension of this, also to be found in Sibelius, is the one-movement symphony, embracing all the contrasts of the orthodox four-movement structure in one broad stream of continuous development.

In view of recent developments, it is probably wiser to think of Sibelius as a final flowering of nineteenth century principles rather than the beginning of anything new.

Along with Sibelius, the most formidable bodies of symphonic work have come from Mahler, Elgar, Nielsen, Vaughan Williams, Serge Prokofiev (1891-1953), Dimitri Shostakovich (1906-1975), and Hans Werner Henze (1926 –   ). The styles they employ range from neo-romanticism to outright atonality, with every shade and variation in between.

Possibly because purely descriptive music has suffered a decline in the twentieth century (there have been few symphonic poems) some composers have made use of both solo and choral voices in their symphonies. In this way they have been able to give their music a specific 'meaning', without falling victim to the dangerous ambiguities of a 'programme'. Examples can be found in the symphonies of Mahler, and in Stravinsky (*Symphony of Psalms*) and Benjamin Britten (*Spring Symphony*).

There has been a considerable increase in the number of free symphonic pieces, consisting either of one extended movement, or of several movements linked in the manner of a suite. Ballet, for example, has enriched the concert repertoire with works of this kind (Stravinsky's *Rite of Spring* and *Petrushka,* Vaughan Williams's *Job,* and Ravel's *Daphnis and Chloe*).

Symphonic works for Chamber Orchestra have also increased in popularity, partly because the twentieth century mind has been drawn to the clear textures of the chamber group, and partly because sheer economics have made large orchestras something of a luxury. For the same reasons the String Orchestra, seldom used in the nineteenth century, has attracted a fine repertoire of modern pieces.

The same considerations have acted in favour of a general revival of chamber music of all kinds, and there is scarcely any combination of instruments that has not attracted at least some attention—even the percussion section has been duly honoured. The century's most important string quartets are probably the six by Bartók.

The solo concerto has also flourished, though with rather less emphasis on empty display than in the latter part of the nineteenth century, and with considerable inroads made on the virtual monopoly of violin and piano as solo instruments. Like the symphony, the concerto has adapted itself to every style, and most important composers have made contributions in this field. Undoubtedly the rise of eminent virtuosi for nearly every instrument, has helped to keep the form in a healthy state.

The general tendency in opera has been for composers to choose their style according to their subject matter. For example, the romantic realism of Puccini called for a continuous orchestral background, spun in mosaic fashion from a number of recurrent themes, against which the voices sing in a perpetual arioso. At times this stream of vocal melody hardens into a definite aria, but there is nothing like the abrupt separation of aria from recitative that existed in earlier opera. Indeed, this blurring over of what had previously been separate ingredients is one of the basic characteristics of all modern opera.

In his expressionist period, Richard Strauss adopted a frankly Wagnerian technique, but in later works he relaxed in favour of a simpler, more vocal style.

Puccini and Strauss, the heirs respectively of Verdi and Wagner, were the last composers to produce a series of operas that immediately became part of the international repertoire. Since their heyday only Benjamin Britten (1913-1976), representing an unexpected revival of English operatic talent, has made any sizeable contribution to Europe's opera houses.

Nevertheless, there have been many successful operas in a multitude of different styles. Neo-classicism, complete with da capo arias and recitatives accompanied by the harpsichord, is represented on the world's stages by Stravinsky's *The Rake's Progress*; atonality by Alban Berg's *Wozzeck* and *Lulu*; the inspiration of folk music is to be seen at its most impressive in the operas of Janáček, and jazz in the work of Kurt Weill.

Economic considerations have even played a part in operatic development, prompting a new form: Chamber Opera—designed for small theatres and a handful of singers and instrumentalists. Benjamin Britten is perhaps the most enterprising explorer in these fields, and his most recent experiments in combining the ritual of the Japanese Noh theatre with elements of the medieval Christian Mystery Play have borne particularly fruitful results.

Composers have continued to write religious music, both for use as part of the church liturgy and for the concert platform—though it must be admitted that the business of providing music for the liturgy has fallen largely into the hands of minor composers. A number of masterpieces have appeared that express, within a general religious framework, a more personal kind of spiritual message: Janáček's *Glagolitic Mass,* and Britten's *War Requiem,* for example. Even professed agnostics, such as Vaughan Williams, have been inspired by the beauty of religious texts and their own sympathy with the revelations of sincere mysticism to produce works that have proved convincing and moving to sceptic and believer alike.

Perhaps the most outstanding contribution to religious music has come from Olivier Messiaen (1908-). Highly chromatic, tonally free harmony, elaborately organised rhythms, intricate melodies (influenced by birdsong), and exotic instrumentation—all contribute to a very personal brand of emotional mysticism, inspired by the Catholic faith.

CHAPTER XXIV

RECENT EXPERIMENTS

SINCE the end of World War II there have been many unusual experiments in music. Though, when set against the wider background of more traditional methods, they must be viewed as minority preoccupations, they are of absorbing interest as signs of the very troubled state that musical style had reached by the middle of the twentieth century.

Contrary to many expectations, atonal methods gained ground among young composers in the late 1940's. The example of Schönberg was generally dethroned in favour of Webern – the remorseless logic of whose intense, fragmentary utterances appealed strongly to a generation in hot pursuit of ultimate truths.

Typical avant-garde music continued the reaction against romantic textures, tonal harmony, thematic continuity, and nearly everything else. Sounds came to be arranged as isolated events in time and space, made meaningful by the unfolding of serial patterns. To the uninitiated listener, worshipping in ever-increasing numbers the music of the past and bombarded by the simplistic appeals of 'pop' music in its various forms, the result seemed, more often than not, merely arbitrary. It suggested little or no sense of musical purpose.

In the 1950's certain composers, notably the Frenchman Pierre Boulez (1925-), the German Karlheinz Stockhausen (1928-), and the Italians Luigi Nono (1924-) and Bruno Maderna (1920-1973), embarked upon experiments in TOTAL SERIALISM in which every element in music – notes, rhythms, dynamics, pitch, and timbre – was organised along serial lines. In doing so they imposed almost impossible demands on performers and brought themselves to the point where it was necessary to consider artificial, scientifically exact ways of producing the effects they envisaged.

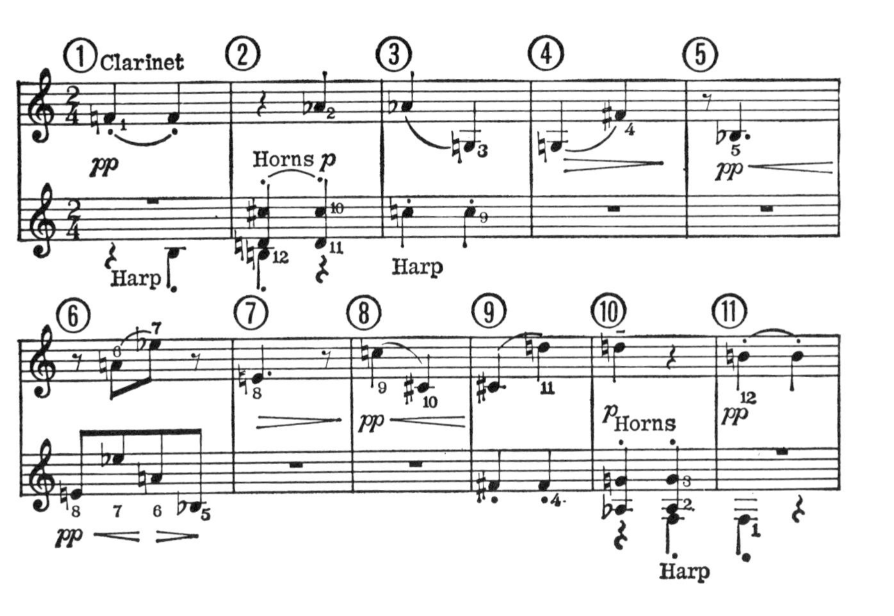

NOTE ROW

Atonality: Webern *Symphony* Op 21—'theme' from second movement variations
The note row appears in the clarinet melody and also, in reverse, in the accompaniment. There are many, typical, ingenious relationships between the melodic phrases—for example: the intervals in bars 11 to 8 (clarinet) are identical with those in bars 1 to 4.

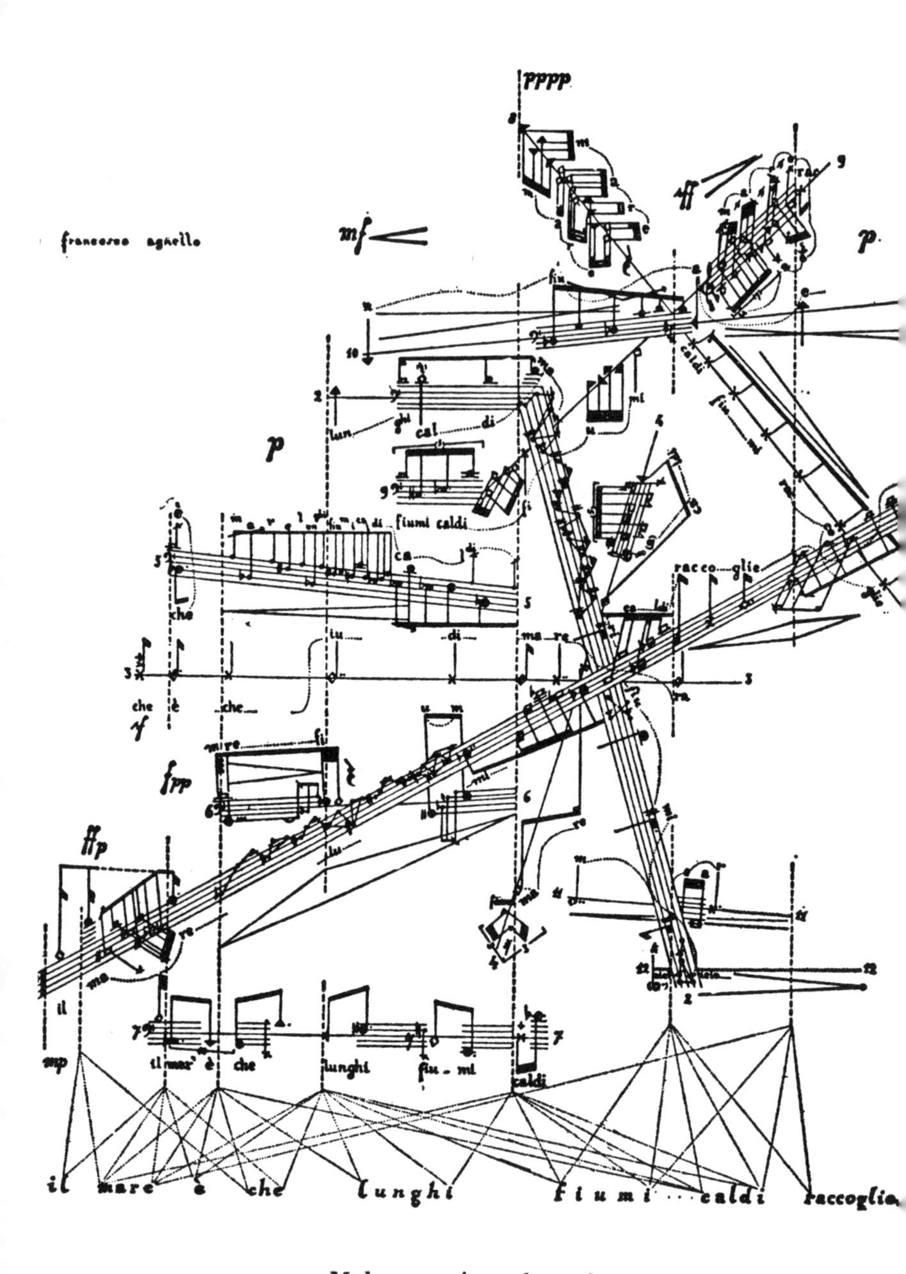

Modern experimental notation:
from Bussotti's Siciliano

Reproduced by permission of Aldo Bruzzichelli Editore, Florence; Exclusive Agents, Hinrichsen Edition, Ltd., London

The development of ELECTRONIC MUSIC, at roughly the same time, was therefore not surprising. In the Electronic Studio composers were able to build up sound patterns of amazing intricacy, recording them direct on to tape and eventually emerging with the finished article – composed and performed in a single process over which they had complete control.

There are two basic approaches to electronic composition. Either the composer can record natural sounds and then mix them in a kind of musical 'collage', or he can take 'pure' sounds, generated by high frequency oscillators, and use these as his basic material. The first method is usually referred to as MUSIQUE CONCRÈTE – a name and technique invented in 1948 by the composer Pierre Schaeffer (1910-). The second, and by far the more fruitful and important method, is known simply as ELECTRONIC MUSIC. In both cases the tape recorder opened up undreamed of possibilities for new sounds – sounds speeded up or slowed down, played backwards, distorted, refined, and endlessly manipulated.

Certain radio stations (notably Paris and Cologne) established elaborate Sound Laboratories in which composers could experiment to their heart's content. The arrival of the SYNTHESIZER and COMPUTER gave added impetus and new dimensions to their work. The year 1977 saw the establishment by Boulez in Paris of the Institut de Recherche et de Coordination Acoustique/Musique (IRCAM) – its sights firmly set upon discovering the 'Music of the Future'. The appeal of appearing scientific in a scientific age was apparently not to be resisted!

Total serialism and electronically produced music both call for a high degree of calculation and, rightly or wrongly, suggest a sense of rigid predetermination. Inevitably a new cult sprang up which took an opposite view: that of INDETERMINACY. Here the maximum liberty was permitted and the laws of chance allowed free reign. Performers were encouraged to improvise, either for short periods during the course of a notated composition, or throughout – using whatever was provided as a 'score' as a means of stimulating their imaginations.

In the latter instance, orthodox musical notation was often abandoned altogether, and 'scores' consisting of some form of GRAPHIC NOTATION (blots and blotches, squiggles and dashes) were used instead. The performer either played whatever his imagination prompted him to play, or settled to the task of learning whatever meaning the composer chose to reveal of the new 'notation'.

Music that thus involved elements of chance came to be described as ALEATORY – a word borrowed from the Latin *alea*, meaning 'dice'. Its chief propagandist was the American John Cage (1912-), who was also associated with the chance effects of the so-called PREPARED

PIANO – an instrument whose sound has been tampered with by the addition of bits and pieces (such as screws and strips of paper) to the strings.

Alongside the unpredictable came music organised according to the most rigorous mathematical principles. STOCHASTIC music, for example, associated with the Greek composer Iannis Xenakis (1922-) – a form of music in which the individual details give the appearance of being random, while their overall progression is in fact determined by the subtle laws of mathematical probability.

By way of reaction against such extremes of intellectual calculation there came, in the late 1960's, the idea of MINIMAL MUSIC, notably in the work of such American composers as Steve Reich (1936-) and Philip Glass (1937-). Here, simple ostinato patterns (arpeggios, brief chord sequences – all usually tonal) are repeated hypnotically over and over again, so that time and 'progression' seem to be defeated, even though, by means of almost imperceptible changes, there is in fact a gradual sense of evolution and forward motion. Such ideas owe much to Indian, African, and Balinese music and stand as evidence of the degree to which the different cultures of the entire world (and indeed of the whole of recorded history) had now come to interact upon each other. This willingness to learn from past or alien cultures is unique to the twentieth-century artist, and though obviously enriching, the sheer diversity of the experience has also proved somewhat bewildering.

To the twentieth century's purely musical explorations must also be added experiments in the semi-theatrical presentation of events, in which HAPPENINGS (musical or otherwise) become an integral part of the performance. MIXED MEDIA events, involving music, drama, visual and verbal elements, challenge the ground formerly possessed by opera, while the idea of SPATIAL MUSIC, in which the physical disposition of the actual forces form part of the composition, call into question the traditional ensemble.

In short, there is nothing in music that the twentieth century has left unchallenged. And although at first sight this condition may seem to argue an age without conviction, it may well be that it is this very breadth of approach that offers the greatest promise for the future.

At all events, there can be no doubt as to the quality and quantity of the music of the period – more, probably, than has been produced in all the previous centuries put together. In addition to those already singled out in this chapter, even the most random selection of twentieth century composers would include the most amazing galaxy of diverse and contradictory talents. Such composers as Luigi Dallapiccola (1904-1975), Michael Tippett (1905-), Witold Lutoslawski

(1913-), György Ligeti (1923-), Toru Takemitsu (1930-), Krzysztof Penderecki (1933-), Peter Maxwell Davies (1934-), Harrison Birtwistle (1934-) and, quite literally, thousands of equally individual and worthwhile talents from every part of the globe have made and are making their contribution. Whatever the stylistic uncertainties of the period, there has been no shortage of creative imagination!

CHAPTER XXV

THE COMPOSER TODAY

WE began this brief account of Europe's music by considering the composer's place in society. Today, although it may be difficult to define the precise role he plays, his position is probably more favourable than at any other time. The business of music publishing is now organised on a large scale, and the composer, for the first time in history, is assured of a legal right to a fair share in the profits. The sale of sheet music may not count for very much, but the royalties from public performance, broadcasting and gramophone records can mount up very handsomely. A successful twentieth-century composer may find himself a very wealthy man or woman.

Moreover, there is hardly anybody who wishes to dictate to him. Private patronage (the little that exists) seldom makes specific demands. Nor do the growing number of semi-public patrons—the orchestras, radio and television companies, and the committees of the innumerable Festivals that have mushroomed in recent years. They will, of course, state the occasion they have in mind and the musical forces they can afford, but they leave the rest to the composer. Only in Soviet Russia, where he is directly and handsomely supported by the State through all stages of his career, is the composer likely to be called to order—but even this totalitarian approach shows signs of relaxing.

The twentieth century composer, then, has much to be thankful for. But he may perhaps regret the curious isolation of his position. At the back of his mind there must now be the uncomfortable suspicion that he is no longer absolutely needed. For the music-loving world is very busy with the masterpieces of the past (an entirely twentieth-century preoccupation, this), and could manage quite well without further additions.

Part of the blame must rest with the composer himself. Starting with the nineteenth-century cult of individuality and the hero-artist, he has too often deliberately set himself apart. He has shown himself contemptuous of appealing to a wide audience, and cannot be surprised if that audience now decides to ignore him. The situation is particularly apparent in the alarming gulf that separates 'pop' from 'serious' music—a state of affairs that did not exist in other centuries in anything like the same acute form.

The circle of mutual distrust has proved a vicious one. Out of it has been bred a new type of composer, bent on proving himself avant-garde at all costs, and concerned to communicate only with a small circle of friends and initiates. It has been left to the twentieth century to elevate the idea of perpetual innovation into a positive way of artistic life.

Fortunately there are still composers who can command a wide popularity without actually courting it. And it would seem likely that it is in their hands that the future of music lies.

NOTES

NOTES

NOTES

NOTES

APPENDIX A

Suggestions for Further Study

The rate at which new books and recordings appear and then disappear has increased so rapidly in recent years that there is now very little point in making, as in the first edition of this book, specific recommendations. The content and approach of these Appendices has therefore been completely revised.

Cassette, longplay, and compact disc recordings are available to cover all the topics suggested in the 'Listening Student's Checklist' section. In tracing them, besides consulting those of the major record companies, the catalogues of such smaller enterprises as Chandos, Hyperion, Lyrita, Nimbus should be considered – for they often touch on areas of music that the larger companies deem uneconomic or unimportant.

So far as books are concerned, what is now recommended are only those publications which are clearly destined for a long shelf-life and which, by definition, are outstanding of their kind. For the consistently high standard of their music book publications the catalogues of the following firms should be consulted: The Oxford University Press, The Cambridge University Press, Faber & Faber, Thames & Hudson, Macmillan and J. M. Dent & Sons, Ltd.

Books

Works of Reference

- *The New Grove Dictionary of Music & Musicians* (20 volumes), ed. Stanley Sadie (Macmillan)
- *The New Oxford Companion to Music* (2 volumes), ed. Denis Arnold (Oxford University Press)
- *The Concise Oxford Dictionary of Music,* ed. Michael Kennedy (Oxford University Press)
- *Twentieth Century Music* (encyclopaedia) by Paul Griffiths (Thames & Hudson)

Histories of Music

- *The New Oxford History of Music* (10 volumes), ed. Gerald Abraham (Oxford University Press)
- *Man and His Music* by Harman, Mellers & Milner (Barrie & Rockliffe)
- *Modern Music: a Concise History* by Paul Griffiths (Thames & Hudson: The World of Art)

Individual Composers
The Master Musician Series (J. M. Dent)
The New Grove: The Composer Biography Series (Macmillan)
Novello Short Biographies (Novello)
The BBC Music Guides (Ariel Books, BBC)

Background Books
A World History of Art by Hugh Honour & John Fleming (Macmillan)
The Oxford Illustrated History of English Literature, ed. Pat Rogers (Oxford University Press)
The Oxford Companion to Literature, ed. Margaret Drabble (Oxford University Press)
An Illustrated History of the World by H. G. Wells, revised by Philip Ziegler (Webb & Bower/Michael Joseph)
The Penguin Atlas of World History (2 volumes) by Hermann Kinder & Werner Hilgemann (Penguin Paperback)

The Listening Student's Checklist

Rather than specify particular works (as was done in the first edition of the Outline History) it has seemed preferable to list, under each separate topic, those composers with whose music the student should try to become acquainted. It cannot be too strongly emphasised that it is the *sound* of music that matters, and that none of the information offered in this book is of the slightest use unless fully related to that sound.

Try not to live by the gramophone alone. A symphony needs to be heard in a concert hall. An opera is almost meaningless unless you can see it staged. Church music belongs in a church acoustic, and folk songs in the village pub. Try always to hear music in its proper place and, better still, try to find ways of joining in its performance.

THE MASS

14th-15th century	Machaut, Dunstable, Josquin des Prés.
16th-17th century	Lassus, Palestrina, Byrd, Tallis.
18th-19th century	J. S. Bach, Haydn, Beethoven, Verdi.
20th century	Janáček, Stravinsky, Britten.

THE PASSION	Schütz, J.S. Bach.

ORATORIO

17th-18th century	Schütz, Handel.
19th century	Mendelssohn.
20th century	Elgar, Tippett.

OPERA	
17th century	Monteverdi, Cavalli, Lully, Purcell.
18th century	Handel, Pergolesi, Gluck, Mozart.
19th century	Bellini, Rossini, Donizetti, Verdi, Weber, Wagner, Moussorgsky.
20th century	Strauss, Debussy, Puccini, Janáček, Berg, Britten, Stravinsky, Tippett.

CHANSON and MADRIGAL	
France	Janequin, Willaert.
Italy	Landini, Giovanni Gabrieli, Monteverdi, Gesualdo
England	Weelkes, Wilbye, Gibbons, Morley.

SOLO SONG	
Germany	Schubert, Schumann, Brahms, Wolf, Strauss.
France	Berlioz, Fauré, Duparc, Poulenc.
England	Dowland, Gurney, Warlock, Finzi, Britten.

SYMPHONY	
18th century	Johann Stamitz, C. P. E. Bach, J. C. Bach, Haydn, Mozart.
19th century	Beethoven, Schubert, Berlioz, Brahms, Dvořák, Tchaikovsky.
20th century	Bruckner, Mahler, Elgar, Rachmaninov, Vaughan Williams, Sibelius, Shostakovich, Tippett, Henze.

CONCERTO GROSSO	Corelli, Handel, J. S. Bach, Vivaldi.

SOLO CONCERTO	
18th century	Mozart.
19th century	Beethoven, Mendelssohn, Liszt, Brahms, Tchaikovsky.
20th century	Berg, Bartók, Prokofiev, Tippett.

SYMPHONIC POEM	Liszt, Strauss, Elgar, Sibelius.
ORGAN MUSIC	J. S. Bach, Reger, Widor, Messiaen.

KEYBOARD MUSIC

17th-18th century	Couperin, Domenico, Scarlatti, Mozart.
19th century	Beethoven, Schubert, Schumann, Chopin, Brahms.
20th century	Debussy, Rachmaninov, Bartók, Messiaen.

STRING QUARTET

18th century	Haydn, Mozart.
19th century	Beethoven, Schubert, Mendelssohn, Brahms.
20th century	Bartók, Shostakovich.

APPENDIX B

Projects

An 'outline' book of this kind cannot be regarded as complete in itself. It provides merely the framework for further, deeper studies. The following projects are offered as examples of the lines along which such studies might be carried out.

1 Using *The New Grove Dictionary of Music and Musicians* and other sources (see Appendix A), collect biographical information about the following composers. In each case compile a short list of their most important compositions:

Medieval	Machaut, Landini
Renaissance	Dunstable, Dufay, Josquin, Lassus, Palestrina, Byrd
Baroque	Monteverdi, Purcell, Lully, Bach, Handel, Vivaldi
Classical	Gluck, Haydn, Mozart, Beethoven, Schubert
Romantic	Mendelssohn, Schumann, Chopin, Liszt, Berlioz, Verdi, Wagner, Brahms, Tchaikovsky, Dvořák
Modern	Debussy, Bartók, Stravinsky, Sibelius, Schönberg, Webern, Shostakovich, Britten, Boulez

2 Make a collection of pictures showing the typical architectural styles of the following periods:
Romanesque, Gothic, Renaissance, Baroque, Rococo, Classical

3 Make a collection of reproductions of typical pictures by the following artists—representatives of their periods:
Giotto, Michelangelo, Titian, Rembrandt, Watteau, Turner, Monet, Picasso

4 Read selections from the work of the following English authors. Think about them as representatives of the style of their time:
Chaucer, Shakespeare, Milton, Dryden, Keats, W. H. Auden

5 Literature has often had a direct influence on music. Find examples of this.

6 Make yourself familiar with the Latin words of the Mass.

7 What would you expect to find in a typical Mass (style, ingredients, etc) at the following approximate dates:
1350, 1450, 1550, 1650, 1750, 1850, 1950

8 What would you expect to find in a typical Symphony at the following approximate dates:
1740, 1790, 1810, 1840, 1890, 1960

9 What would you expect to find in a typical Concerto at the following approximate dates:
1740, 1790, 1810, 1890, 1960

10 List the basic ingredients (the kind of overture, aria, recitative, the use of chorus, ensemble, and orchestra) in operas by the following composers:
Monteverdi, Purcell, Handel, Gluck, Mozart, Verdi, Wagner, Puccini, Britten

11 What kinds of solo song existed in: 1400, 1600, 1800, 1960? Who sang such songs, and on what occasions? Name typical composers.

12 Name typical dances of: 1500, 1600, 1750, 1850, 1960.

13 Find works that make use of the following musical devices:
The idée fixe, Metamorphosis of themes, Leitmotiv, Motto theme, Cyclic unity, The Note Row, Indeterminacy.

14 What kinds of music depended upon 'points of imitation', in the 16th century, 17th century, 18th century?

15 Who would have been in charge of the performance of:
a Mass in the 15th century; a Symphony in the 18th century; a Symphony in the late 19th century?

16 What were the dominant musical forms (ie Mass, Symphony Concerto, etc) in the years: 1500, 1650, 1750, 1850, 1950?

17 What were the social conditions of the composer in 1500, 1700, 1800, 1900? Who did he work for, and how did he earn his living?

18 What kind of music would the ordinary man in the street have enjoyed and been provided with in: 1500, 1600, 1700, 1800, 1960?

19 Find out the names of composers associated with the Nationalist Movements in Russia, Bohemia, Scandinavia, Germany, Italy, Spain, and England. For each composer find a work that expresses their nationalist sympathies.

20 What instruments would you find in a typical orchestra of 1600, 1720, 1790, 1820, 1880?

21 Build up a table of ranges for the following groups of instruments:
the lute, the classical guitar, the harp
the violin, the viola, the cello
the trumpet, the French horn, the trombone
the organ, the harpsichord, the piano.

22 How many strings would you expect to find on the classical guitar, the lute, the viola da gamba, the banjo, the double bass?

23 Collect information (including pictures) about the history and mechanics of the following instruments:
Virginals, Clavichord, Harpsichord, Fortepiano, Pianoforte

24 Examine the first movements of the following works, as examples of sonata-allegro form:
Mozart's *Eine kleine Nachtmusik,* Beethoven's *Fifth Symphony,* Dvořák's *New World Symphony*

25 The following works, typical of their period, both make use of sonata-allegro form for their first movements. They arrange the ingredients differently, however. Find out what the differences are.
Mozart's Piano Concerto in A major, K.488
Mendelssohn's Violin Concerto in E minor

26 Find examples in a Concerto Grosso, a Da Capo Aria, an oratorio chorus, of the use of the Ritornello Principle.

27 Examine closely one of Bach's fugues from the '48'—for example, No 9 in E major, from Book II. How many times does he use the Subject and Answer? Can you find examples of stretto, diminution, inversion?

28 Although they tell a story, the following works also have a logical musical form:
Strauss's *Don Juan,* Tchaikovsky's *Romeo & Juliet* Overture.
What are these forms?

29 The Slow Introduction to a symphony often gives the impression that the composer is 'searching for a theme', which he then uses in the sonata-allegro that follows. Examine the

first movement of Haydn's Symphony No 102, in B flat major. What is the connecting link between the theme of the slow introduction (Eulenberg miniature score page 1), the first subject (p 3) and the second subject (p 8)?

30 What kinds of scales, and what kinds of harmony would you expect to find in music at 1400, 1500, 1700, 1800, 1880, 1960?

Obviously there is no end to the avenues through which a deeper study of music can be approached, and the wise student will not rest content with the suggestions offered in this appendix. He might, for example, take short pieces of music from different periods and arrange them for whatever instruments he and his friends can muster.

But whatever he does, he should try always to approach the subject without prejudice and without too many pre-conceived notions about what music should or should not be. Music is written by human beings, and for human beings. Text books are merely aids towards a better understanding of what must first be *enjoyed* for its own sake.

INDEX

GCSE
MUSIC PROJECTS
LET'S MAKE MUSIC
TREVOR WEBB AND NICHOLAS DREWE
Let's Make Music is a series of five books giving practical projects for use in preparations for the GCSE examination in music.
1: Let's Begin
2: Let's Go On
3: Let's Listen
4: Let's Listen Again
5: Let's Compose
PLUS Answer Book
ALSO AVAILABLE
Teacher's Pack including
Books 1-5 and an Answer Book
All five books are grounded positively on the three major principles of the GCSE syllabi: listening, composing and performing.
LET'S MAKE MUSIC
aims to teach skills not facts
encourages active participation and self-criticism from pupils
illustrates new concepts with a wide range of musical and visual examples
provides a variety of different technical topics ensuring a progressive approach to learning
TO THE TEACHER
This series is aimed at pupils in the 13 plus age-group and the topics selected have been carefully chosen to have a wide appeal and application in schools. The intention is that those who are interested in all kinds of music, but not necessarily learning an instrument, will derive some pleasure and measured achievement from active participation in the subject.
Novello